RENATO SALVI
ARCHITECT

RENATO SALVI
ARCHITECT

BIRKHÄUSER
BASEL

Collection Archigraphy Lémaniques. This collection, which simultaneously covers historical and theoretical fields, pursues the objectives of publishing the complete works of contemporary architects, and thus incorporating documentation for the founding of a critical reflection relating to the evolution of architectural practice in Switzerland.
Collection Archigraphy Lémaniques is directed by Bruno Marchand.

Introduction

Part 1: Infrastucture

Part 2: Architecture

> Public Buildings

> Private Villas

> Renovations

Appendix

BRUNO MARCHAND

The Architect's Audacity

Interview with Renato Salvi

9:18 a.m. Cutting past the craggy cliffs of the impressive Moutier gorge, where a few fingers of fog linger on, the ICN 617 train to Basel finally stops in the capital of the Swiss Jura: Delémont. After a brief crossing through a rather dull and desolate plain, the arrival at the train station is full of surprises: the walk down from the platforms leads you to an underground passage that is unexpectedly luminous (thanks to an ingenious shifting of the footbridge between the two platforms) and framed by inclined lateral walls covered in sheet metal, the whole topped by an extremely low ceiling no higher than two meters.

The visitor is thus guided by this "carved out" space that unfurls itself lengthwise, lit on either side by horizontal luminous bands that reflect onto the walls and ceiling. Rising up toward the main hall of the train station, I am dazzled for a brief moment by the discovery of a high space, covered with a generous metallic roof and modeled by a series of stairs that lead, in a very comfortable and spacious manner, either toward the town centre or to platform number one.

It is rare that the train station of a small town should be endowed with such a wonderful architectural promenade; a promenade which becomes urban by unfolding in the direction of the parking area under a covered passage, with about eighty meters of retail or simply window-shopping opportunities for the traveler. All of these developments and spaces, of great quality, are the fruit of the work of Renato Salvi, a Delémont-based architect who has welcomed me here for this interview.

Bruno Marchand — *What made you set up base in Delémont?*

Renato Salvi — I arrived in Delémont by chance and have been based here permanently since 1988, after winning the competition for the Transjurane highway with Flora Ruchat-Roncati. Nothing in my career path had predestined me for this, however. I'm of Italian origins and was born in La Chaux-de-Fonds – an austere town in the north of Switzerland, with a harsh climate, which suits me well. My father was a mason who immigrated to Switzerland in the 1950s and my mother worked in the watch industry. This family model exposed me simultaneously to the tough reality of the construction site, and to the precise and patient work required of watchmaking.

◀ R. SALVI, NUDE, WATERCO-
LOR (2004)

BM — *A family model and context that really left its mark…*

RS — Absolutely. We can make some amusing parallels. The context is that of a town that is aesthetically powerful in its repetitions: its identical windows, identical staircases, its similarly equipped kitchens, etc. On the other hand, you have watch mechanisms that can be taken apart, that are also often identical and repetitive. Repetition seems to be the key word: the movement of watches is always the same, made up of a number of components; it is the variations in the movement that distinguish one watch from another.

BM — *Something changed, however, after you decided to study in Zurich.*

RS — My departure for the Swiss Federal Institute of Technology (ETH) in Zurich in 1981 to study architecture confronted me for the first time with a cosmopolitan context and more importantly made me discover an intellectual field that I was instantly attracted to. Even if, in a way, I managed to "escape" the influence of Aldo Rossi that was still prevalent at that time and that, I must admit, I never fully grasped.
At the ETH, Bernhard Hoesli taught the first year of studies and left his mark on successive generations of architects by introducing us to modernity. The way he approached this topic really spoke to me. But I lived the most memorable experience in my third year: the charting of the Fez Medina for five months under the direction of the invited professor Stefano Bianca, funded by UNESCO. For me, this was the discovery of incredible Moroccan towns and an introduction to both vernacular architecture and to another culture, grounded in other values.
Last but not least, Flora Ruchat-Roncati's teaching was certainly a central point in my studies. She combines a rational approach with a humanist spirit, both in her perception of things and toward architecture. I still remember her description of how to plant an orchard in pentagonal form so that each tree might have sun. There's always something innovative and creative behind her seemingly trivial words: that is the Flora that I have always appreciated. This affinity led me to work in her Rome office for almost four years after my studies, splitting my time between the office and a building restoration course that I followed assiduously, although I must admit the latter didn't mark my career.

BM — *How was your time in Rome significant for you?*

RS — It was a way of going back to my roots and rediscovering them in a surprising way. I still vividly recall the atmosphere of a particular sun-soaked Italian plaza, or waiting for a bus right next to an archeological park, or coming across a fresco in a museum. Also the feeling of confronting – for the first time – a non-dogmatic interpretation of modernity, free in its choice of materials and how they are presented, in the style of the architect Luigi Moretti. He was an intriguing character who had an ability to somehow resurface over time. His thirties work fascinates me but he also built things in an extremely free manner in the fifties, after having spent time in jail. It's crazy and strange.

BM — *So you were interested in both a return to traditional architecture and also modern Italian works, including the complex architecture of Luigi Moretti as highlighted by Robert Venturi?*

RS — Yes, the obvious complexity of the Palazzina Il Girasole interests me, but what I like the most is that in it you can see an architectural form that could be called sensual. A sensuality created by the materials, the textures, the atmosphere, which are always changing with the light. A form of sensuality that one also feels when you touch a concrete wall by Scarpa, a gesture that always gives me a thrill. Speaking of which, I remember Bernhard Hoesli, who would let his fingers linger on the bare concrete of La Tourette and say: "Drawing architectural plans is not enough, you have to touch the material!" Scarpa also moves me in the relationship he established with landscape and natural elements. I'm thinking of the cemetery wall of the Brion family at San Vito d'Altivole, which is at the exact same height as that of the cornstalks growing in the adjacent field. He also had a refined approach to detail.

▼ R. SALVI, BOUCA COMPLEX BY A.
SIZA, PEN AND INK SKETCH (1986)

▼ R. SALVI, QUINTA DA CONCEIÇÃO SWIMMING
POOL BY A. SIZA, PEN AND INK SKETCH (1986)

BM — *What other references feed your imagination?*

RS — On the one hand, I would have to mention Alvaro Siza who I discovered when I was a student and who instantly fascinated me, both in terms of his canonic works like the Leça swimming pool and by the tightly linked exterior staircases in the social housing complex of the Bouça in Porto, an image like no other that is both incredibly lively and fascinating, with all those people going up and down those stairs. On the other hand there's Alvar Aalto, whose work I visited much later on a trip with Jean-Claude Girard, who was working with me at the time. I was delighted to have visited Aalto when I was more, let's say, mature, because his architecture is not easy to understand. Notably due to the profusion of materials he uses, his particular way of putting them together, of "telescoping" them out, in a creative form that could almost be destabilizing but actually isn't.

Of course, both of these architects are very much in touch with nature and landscape. This theme is particularly interesting to me and brings me back to my own background and to Italian landscapes: returning to my

▲ R. SALVI, JYVASKYLA UNI-
VERSITY BY A. AALTO, PENCIL
SKETCH (1996)

village, crossing through the great Po Valley, arriving at the foot of Bergamo with its old town, going up into the village, with its hills, to find another type of vegetation, the softness of this landscape in comparison to the Swiss forests, etc. There is something nourishing in this vision of landscape.

BM — *Let's come back to your career. It seems evident to me that it is atypical compared to most architects of your generation because you spent over ten years drawing and implementing this incredible infrastructure that is the Transjurane highway, after winning the competition in 1988 with Flora Ruchat-Roncati. This effectively allowed you to confront landscape in a very direct manner.*

RS — That's right, for ten years or more the drawing and implementation of the Transjurane was a key part of my daily activities and in a certain way it "froze" my work as an architect. During that period I simply had neither the time nor the energy to take on other construction sites or architectural projects. But the Transjurane was an exceptional and unusual experience because it did not necessarily imply spatial research. It was more about the art of placing objects in a landscape, giving these objects a certain sculptural quality. It's a memorable experience that has stayed with me since I started my own company in 1998.

BM — *Let's talk about form and its significance in your projects.*

RS — There's a sentence by Marguerite Yourcenar that I really like: "I really must concern myself with form, form is what distinguishes me from my dog." I belong to a generation of architects where, for a long time, any vague attempt at form was condemned. It took many years for me to rid myself of this pressure, which is fundamentally paradoxical because, for any architect, the formal approach is the primary basis of his or her work – undoubtedly drawing architecture into the field of sculpture. For me, the work on the highway was key because it allowed me to create very sculptural objects that are not necessarily autonomous: their form depends on a certain number of parameters, such as context, functionality, etc. But not on these alone...

BM — *It seems to me that the formal approach is a common thread in your work and, in that way, creates a link between infrastructural and architectural elements. Most notably in the search for pure and simple forms that are also radical in their expression. I'm thinking of the Porrentruy school in particular with its two lateral walls and an exposed concrete cantilever, or even the powerful cantilever on the terrace of the Saignelégier villa.*

RS — Yes, that's right, I always try to reach the most exact form, notably in relation to the landscape. In this way a dialogue is created, sometimes with surprising facets: when I think of the Montavon Villa, it is not an architectural form that cuts through the landscape but rather the landscape that cuts through the house. I really take into account the relation to landscape when I evaluate how architectural objects that I'm drawing will be implanted into these sites. In this vision of things, the small wall at the Paumier Villa is fundamental in the way that it extends itself at ground level and thus defines the garden area.

BM — *Despite its apparent fragility, this constructed element gives a certain power and strength to the house.*

RS — I appreciate you using the term fragility, because I do believe that there are some fragile aspects to my architecture, or seemingly fragile, because perhaps it is this paradox that gives my work a certain strength. Yes, surprisingly. This makes me think of the hillside house, with its walls that seem to come out of the ground, that start from zero and rise up, transforming themselves into a house, and successively become an overhanging roof, the hood, etc. When you see these walls on site, it all seems both fragile and very powerful.

Even the highway has a fragile and a powerful side, which is further revealed with time. The theme of aging, which I discovered in Italy, particularly inspires me. I like this dimension of time passing and confounding certainties. You can feel the weight of time when you look at the Caracalla thermal baths in Rome, but they're also incredibly contemporary. I also find the visual trace of time wonderful, like in the Les Gripons stretch of the highway where moss grows and where the trees have coated the walls with rust.

▼ R. SALVI, THE BATHS OF CARACALLA, WATERCOLOR (1997)

BM — *What other aspects interest you during the project phase?*

RS — I place a great emphasis on how the building is approached, which I visualize as a cinematic sequence or the telling of a story that could be put into words like this: you approach the building and you start to take possession of the entrance, little by little. You go inside, you come across light... Also during the implantation phase – and this is always related to the landscape – I always try to leave the land practically untouched, and to lay my construction down to the nearest centimeter.

BM — *When we look at all the houses you have built, there seems to be no recurring language, despite the prevalent use of stucco walls and exposed concrete.*

RS — For me, the choice of materials is never fixed but varies depending on the circumstances. Let's take the Paumier Villa for example. For quite some time, I imagined it in visible brick, perhaps because Jean-Claude Girard and I had just returned from a trip to Denmark, quite impressed by the architecture of Arne Jacobsen. In the end, the house became white stucco, mostly for financial reasons. Yes, a brick house would have been fantastic in this landscape. But this way of building would not have been appropriate in the context of the Jura where, traditionally, homes are not built of brick.

It is true that, first and foremost, I'm looking for a meaningful way to combine mass and gravity. It's interesting because I think that I only drew one metallic structure in my life, during my studies. I'm pretty sure that it's a technique I don't know very well and that I could only apply to something ephemeral... The mass, which once again takes me back to my origins, is necessary to me, on the one hand to find the sensual part of architecture that we were speaking about before – notably on an acoustic level – and to reach the opposite effects of spatial introversion or extraversion that are often characteristic of my work.

BM — *What is your view of other artistic fields such as painting and sculpture?*

RS — Sometimes, a painting or a sculpture can be almost more meaningful to me than architecture. Ultimately I need an artistic and cultural context in order to feed my imagination as an architect. Last summer I was in Matera where I discovered underground rock churches with frescoes strongly influenced by the Byzantine era – they truly moved me.

These constructions have been there for centuries and there is a kind of Christ-like figure that still gazes out at you compassionately. And we still don't know who painted him, how it happened, why it happened, in that place, how it was made. In that space, on a fresco on a piece of wall in the bottom of a cave, we find a primary need to show something deeper and broader than the human condition.

Zoran Music is a painter that I really appreciate. He died a few years ago and had lived in the concentration camps. He would draw bodies grouped together, using just a stub of pencil and a scrap of paper, and managed to survive in what must have been one of the darkest periods imaginable. Other painters also fascinate me, not only because of their powerful lines but also with their use of colors. I'm thinking specifically about Nicolas de Staël's Sicilian landscapes where he was able to create such striking effects with only three or four colors. I could also mention Coghuf, a sculptor and painter from the Jura, who I particularly like. I must admit that I'm a bit out of step with contemporary art, which does not always move me – although I'm interested in it as an intellectual approach for widening my horizons, making me think differently, off my usual track.

Coming back to the question of relationships between various artistic disciplines, to me painting is vital for architects because it looks for a way to express things. I sometimes feel that architects express themselves through drawing, and the better you can draw, the more capable you are of understanding a certain reality. With this in mind, you could say that being a master at plans, sections, etc. is essential to the creation of interesting objects.

BM — *Let's also talk about literature...*

RS — Reading is definitely a source of inspiration, perhaps because it provides a certain atmosphere that can be brought into the building of a wall or in the drawing of a new space. In speaking about painting, Marguerite Yourcenar really moves me. She describes a farmer who began to pray when he came upon a Christ-figure by Rembrandt. If I had to curate a show I would certainly be inspired by that image and that description, for all that it evokes of the human condition.

Reading helps me to interiorize or to look deep inside of me for things that are hidden away and that I don't fully grasp. All the more so because after having created an object I often feel I didn't really make it. In fact, I have a hard time imagining that that highway is a work that I created over so many years. That this truly gigantic thing could have come from a table, three chairs, and three people huddled together in a small office, you see... it's almost unreal.

BM — *Let's finish this interview with a phrase by the philosopher José Gil that you like to quote: "To have the audacity to live from the audacity of a singular thought." How can we talk about you in terms of audacity, the architect's audacity?*

RS — Audacity lies in a personal attitude, often in relation to working conditions. My living and working "on the fringe" – compared to other urban centers such as Basel, Geneva, or Zurich – involves all forms of resistance to which the architect must confront him or herself. Resistance is often linked to cultural aspects that come out of a conservative setting or are inherently linked to local traditions.
When I think about the highway, the audacity lies in having actually resisted the inertia of people who don't move or who simply don't want things to change. Audacity is also about counteraction: to be at the same time not entirely certain about what you are suggesting but also to believe in a project over the long term, as was the case with the highway. The audacity also lies in knowing how to say no: no I don't agree with you, that's not the way it should be done, it should be done differently. If you don't live with a certain audacity, I don't think you can make bold and daring architecture.

Infrastructure

MARTIN STEINMANN | ## The Repetition of Gestures
Notes on one aspect of Renato Salvi's work for the Transjurane highway

In 1987, the Swiss Canton of Jura announced a competition for two tunnel portals for the planned N16 highway, which would link the canton's various valleys. Up until then, the roads led over mountaintops, which restricted communications between the valleys as well as the economic development of areas located at the fringe of the Swiss plateau. Consequently, the new highway would not only serve the purpose of facilitating easier and faster connections, it would contribute to shaping the very identity of the canton. The Canton of Ticino served as an example: in collaboration with the architect Rino Tami, the highway was given an identity or "face" through uniformly designed structures. In the Ticino example, recurring design elements appear on several occasions – in the form of bridges, walls, and tunnel portals – effectively creating a single structure over several dozen kilometers in length.

But a highway is not just one big *structure*, it is also one big *machine*, which can be clearly seen on the construction sites before all the utilities disappear under concrete or soil. Marked in green, only the exits will hint at the tunnels and installations necessary for running this type of infrastructure. There are certain devices, however, that have a direct impact on portal design. For example, one of them serves to prevent exhaust fumes expired from one tunnel being sucked into another, thanks to an integral portal design element: a wall of a certain length that divides the two traffic lanes at the tunnel exit. We will discuss this further below, but first let us return to the competition.

Renato Salvi, son of an Italian immigrant mason, had settled down in Delémont a few months prior to the competition announcement, having worked with Flora Ruchat-Roncati in Rome, then in Zurich – and also as her assistant at the ETH. With Ruchat-Roncati, Salvi was selected to participate in the competition. As Ruchat-Roncati was still his superior at the ETH, and so as to avoid any legal issues, they developed a joint design proposal that won them the competition. In all, they built a total of three different portal types. Salvi was thirty-two years old at the time and worked directly in Delémont for the highway project, traveling to Zurich when necessary for discussions with Ruchat-Roncati. As of 1998, he became solely responsible for the project, which has yet to be completed: one section and two tunnels remain under construction.

◀ BANNE WEST
(OISELIER)

I mean to show here that the highway will have been an integral part of Salvi's life for at least twenty-five years once the last section is completed, and not just his professional life. Over the course of this period, his ideas have evolved, along with his working conditions: engineers at the contracted firms have changed over time, different firms were engaged for different aspects, and each engineer had his or her own opinion about the proper shape of a bridge, for example. For all of these reasons, Salvi has never ceased to explain and re-explain his ideas. When you listen to Salvi talk about his work for the highway, in an Ajoie inn for example, you can sense a certain weariness.

Throughout all these years, he also kept up a whole other activity, based on what an architect might get in a region like the Jura: a school, a railway station, an office building, and, most often, villas. These all demand quite another level of detailed attention than what would seem necessary for a highway structure, limited to a more simple design as would be appropriate for this type of engineering project. And yet, a change in shuttering panels, from one portion to the next, can also require detailed attention. Salvi raised this point with me on a construction site: this change impacted the effect of the lateral walls, which had been designed as an entity. Although one may not notice this detail when exiting a tunnel at one hundred kilometers per hour, I can understand his disappointment: it affects the integrity of the architectural scheme. And that is what his work on the highway is all about: a scheme, made up of just a few "words" or forms, that allows each different structure to be seen as part of a whole.

In 1988, I joined the collective that was publishing *FACES* in Geneva. The magazine was being reorganized at the time and the first issue – no. 11, 1989 – was devoted to the theme of the *autoroute*, or highway, following the award for the construction of four Transjurane highway portals. In a short article, I attempted to categorize some of the submitted proposals from the standpoint of "form" and "sign." The proposals from the Ruchat-Roncati and Salvi working group, which won the first prize, fell into the "form" category – in the Gestalt sense, taking shape or designed. What I mean by this is that these portals did not attempt to convey meaning by alluding to familiar structures; their meaning was directly derived from their form, as a form of expression.

Before moving on to a short discussion of the N16, I would like to mention the aim of the competition. It was defined as follows by the cantonal architect, in the same issue: when asked whether the structures were designed as a "family," Berry Luscher answered, "The

strength of the project lies in the idea of having a parental relationship between all the objects." This applies to the view from the outside, from other roads – "on the county road, we will see the structures from afar, as is the case in Ticino" – but also from the inside, of sorts, from the point of view of the motorist. "We made a kind of Pascal's wager: does the motorist see the highway and, if so, in what way? And then we thought to ourselves – and herein lies the wager – that the repetition of identical gestures would create the perception." So the forms that are perceived *en passant*, or in passing, would fit together by repetition to give an impression of the road as a whole.

For the competition, Ruchat-Roncati and Salvi developed a typology that could be used on the different site locations. In their descriptions they wrote, "The study attempts to define a formal and structural founding principle... for all of the sites under development. It is therefore not intended as a way to solve a list of problems, case by case." The principle lay in bringing together the sections – portals and central stations – in way that was economical and simple, and to intervene in the landscape as little as possible. They describe the basis of the uniform portal as follows: "Similar technical conditions in all the central stations, air capturing devices of the same dimension, noise-proof panels of similar dimension. The Terri station type is chosen as a baseline, only its air vents will be adapted [to the different types of terrain, M.S.]. Compact air-capturing system, with flexibility in fixing its inclination depending on the site."

The competition was for the Mont-Terri and Mont-Russelin tunnels, whose portals are located in very different terrains: one on the rocky slope of Les Gripons, the other on a gentle slope, which is the more standard terrain for the N16. The models submitted show the inward and outward ventilation shafts for the central section coming together as one flat entity that leans forward much like a visor over the two tunnels. For one, the element follows the slope, and for the other, it juts out at an angle in relation to the topography. The architects use this "Terri Type," which was to vary depending on the terrain, in an attempt to give an expressive form to the tunnel, seen as an event. But they abandoned this concept in the course of their later work in favor of another "type" where the parts would be separated. This was intended to provide a basis for the other portals, with the exception of the Les Gripons basin, where the St-Ursanne entrance and exit form a sort of full-scale Carrera racetrack.

In its built form, the "Terri Type" consists of lateral walls rising in line with the slope to form a ceiling over the two tunnels. A V-shaped "gutter" is placed on these walls and widens nearer to the top, then turns at a right angle to form the peak of the ceiling. The wall between the tunnels starts a little lower down, which means that the "gutter" unites the two. The central station appears a bit further on, like some sort of strange flower that might be found growing in a meadow. This type can be used when the starting point of the tunnels is of the same height, which occurs in only two instances on the N16. Everywhere else, the tunnels are staggered in relation to each other, because the highway comes up against the slant of the valley. Other solutions had to be found for these portals, as can be seen in the later development of Salvi's work. The portals become simpler, not only for topographical reasons, but for financial ones as well. However, I argue, they are all the more powerful.

Driving through the Swiss motorways, you can't help but agree with Luscher: these highways are usually quite terrible. On the one hand, because they were based on incoherent decisions, which lead to a lack of all relationship between forms; and on the other, because most of those decisions were limited to strictly technical requirements. It would be tempting to compare the effect of different portals here, ranging from holes that are merely cut out of the rock and concrete or stone tubes, to the Leventina motorway portals all set in a steep, rocky terrain, with protruding supports for roadway, flat ceilings, and lateral walls that are broken down into a grid of triangular forms. Their perceptual impact is based on the tensions that arise from such forms.

▼ RUSSELIN SOUTH
  (GLOVELIER)
▼ TERRI SOUTH
  (LES GRIPONS)

Tensions also determine the impact of the portals on the Transjurane highway, and mostly for those that Salvi designed on his own. They can be summarized in but a few elements: embankments, walls, ceilings, etc. Because of their great simplicity, these elements create a much more powerful effect that the older ones, and this effect is based on the more-or-less-defined movement of their forms. The "Terri Type" gutters, which look like cardboard, are replaced by seemingly solid wedges. Thus, the lateral walls retreat powerfully backward to the ceiling, whose peak folds into two edges, one narrow and the other large; the former, facing upward, and the latter, facing downward into the tunnel. These two opposing forces give the tunnel a form or shape that expresses, in a very immediate manner, its penetration into the slope of the mountain – a form, therefore, that acknowledges the fact that it is being perceived en passant.

The face of a highway can be defined by the rules that are discerned in its structure. "Civil engineering structures do not need to be works of art. In fact, this is not the case in Ticino. The bridges that cross over the highway are simple bridge beams. However, the abutments are designed in a homogenous fashion, based on a predetermined idea of the nature of these bridges. That is how the highway gives the impression of forming a unity. It is this impression that is important, and not the civil engineering structure in particular," stated engineer Meen in the same issue of *FACES*. "Yet, those responsible for building the N16 were inspired by the reflections developed in Ticino," I wrote at the time. "In this sense, there is an undeniable political facet to their intention: to create a sense of unity in the territory crossed by the highway. And the competition for the portals served this goal precisely: to give a unique face to this highway."

The Transjurane highway portals therefore spark a sense of movement. This is mostly due to the front sections of the openings that are inclined in different ways or, even, are inclined forward or backward to create a tension. But when traveling at eighty or one hundred kilometers per hour, who is likely to see the fold that divides the peak of the ceiling? And yet, this fold does contribute to the highway's expressive quality; and this applies to other things as well, such as the walls and embankments, which are also inclined. Through repetitions, these elements provide the *basso continuo* for the motorist's experience during his or her journey. To achieve this effect, the design elements are based on simple rules. The purpose is to make visible, through structural things, the surrounding landscape – in, for example, the rising and falling of lateral walls, the slope that is being embraced.

▲ BANNE WEST
(OISELIER)
▲ THE ROCHE ST-JEAN
PORTAL

As I have said, the portals have an impact as a form, not as a sign. However, even a sign cannot help but be expressed. The tunnels, as represented on road signals, are given meaning through the image of an arch, bracing against something. Everything is expressive, wrote Rudolf Arnheim, just as much a line as the human body,[1] and all forms of expression are perceived as a form of behavior. That is to say that we perceive the qualities of a form as forces. Perception, as Arnheim said quite acutely, is the experience of visual forces.[2] We perceive a tunnel's arch – or at least the sign that represents it – as something stable, while we perceive the aforementioned front-section walls as unstable. This tunnel opening leans forward and is filled with a tension that we perceive as movement. Luscher is therefore quite justified in calling these portals *des gestes*, or gestures.

A construction has a spontaneous meaning if, in its form, it conveys qualities that are relevant to us.[3] What would then be the significance of the forward-inclined western tunnel portal of Banné, to use a typical example? Not only does it lean forward in a very forceful fashion and in the direction of the motorist, but it also becomes heavier near the front, creating an all the more violent sense of movement. The strong tension expressed through its form makes the slope of the mountainside all the more visible, as if the slope had deformed the wall. Indeed, this distortion of such a simple form, the vertical opening, acts as a catalyst for tension.[4] This tension is also evident in the ceiling of the tunnel. But the lateral walls, which rise toward the tunnel, becoming broader – and thicker – work against this movement, so that ultimately the visual forces are brought into equilibrium, without canceling each other out; as we drive toward the portal, they are discernible as opposing movements.

Examining every portal through the angle of all the diverse visual combinations they represent would be going too far. These few notes will have to suffice for showing the main approach used by Salvi for revealing the highway as one dynamic entity. The form deviates from the vertical, inclines forward, backward or to the side, etc. As mentioned above, we perceive all of these forms as types of behavior; that is why we use verbs to describe their different aspects, that is why they are expressive, and that expressiveness – to borrow again from Arnheim – is to be defined as modes of behavior that are revealed through the appearance of things in motion.[5]

One could object and say that the lateral walls that lean against the slope are there for static reasons. Certainly, but Salvi integrated this technical constraint – and others – into a repertoire of forms that define the expression of the portals as a whole. They are simple forms, as is appropriate for road building. (After the first portals, there was a radicalization.) Salvi combines them to create structures where each part, through its properties, fits in with the dynamic of the whole. A dynamic that also includes the landscape, as I have shown, that we perceive even more consciously because of the portals. The lateral wall of the Roche St-Jean tunnel, pointing steeply upward, gives us a sense of the confined nature of the cluse, while the Neu Bois tunnel, stretching forward, evokes the vast expanses of the Ajoie plateau.

With what is essentially a simple set of rules, Salvi has succeeded in designing portals in very different terrains that share an intimate formal relationship. A list of the "cases" – there are four or five – reveals the rules, but also the way in which they are actually deployed in relation to the particular characteristics of each site location. Space is lacking to address that here. Besides, certain sites are still under construction, as I said at the start. Corn still covers some of the fields that the highway will one day pass through. And therefore a text on these portals – and on the highway in general – may be a bit premature. There is one aspect that can not as yet be discerned, and that is the relationship between the highway and landscape once all of the machines will have left their construction sites, once the lanes are cloaked in asphalt all along the N16, and once the embankments are covered with grass... in short, once the highway becomes an integral part of the valleys that make up the Jura.

1 Rudolf Arnheim, Kunst und Sehen – Eine Psychologie des schöpferischen Auges, Berlin 1978, p. 455
2 Ibid., p. 414
3 Rudolf Arnheim, Dynamik der architektonischen Form, Cologne 1980, p. 214
4 Rudolf Arnheim, Kunst und Sehen, op. cit. p 422
5 Ibid., p. 448

BONCOURT FRANCE

PORRENTRUY WEST
Banné West
Banné East
Perche West
Perche East
Viaduct Voyeuboeuf
PORRENTRUY EAST

ST-URSANNE

DELÉMONT WEST

DELÉMONT EAST

MOUTIER

SECTIONS 1-2

SECTION 3

SECTIONS 4-5-6

SECTION 7

SECTION 8

The highway as landscape

Working on an infrastructure such as a highway immediately prompts the question of relation to landscape. One tactic might have been to try to conceal the development in order to minimize its visual impact on sites that are considered to be part of the natural environment. Quite another approach was adopted: the highway was conceived and constructed as a contemporary asset, with its own scenic value. A highway is a historic construction and as a testament of our times it brings an additional dimension to a landscape. The idea was to stand out from and fit into an existing context, rather than simply blend in. The entrances to the Voyeboeuf and Oiselier tunnels are staggered to avoid artificially creating a central dividing wall, characteristic of similar civil engineering structures. They were positioned in such a way that the surrounding land could be returned to its original condition, after the intervention.

◀ BANNE EAST
▼ PERCHE WEST

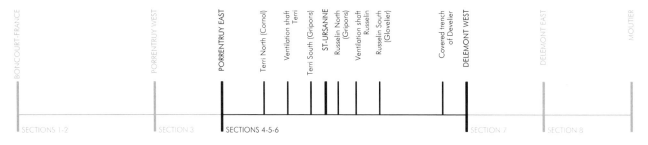

BONCOURT-FRANCE

PORRENTRUY WEST

PORRENTRUY EAST

Terri North (Cornol)

Ventilation shaft
Terri

Terri South (Gripons)

ST-URSANNE

Russelin North
(Gripons)

Ventilation shaft
Russelin

Russelin South
(Glovelier)

Covered trench
of Develier

DELEMONT WEST

DELEMONT EAST

MOUTIER

SECTIONS 1-2

SECTION 3

SECTIONS 4-5-6

SECTION 7

SECTION 8

▼ TERRI SOUTH (LES GRIPONS)

Elaborating a language

A connection to the landscape was established through the development
of a unifying language for all the civil engineering constructions on the
highway — from the simple lower underpass railings to the upper passageways, embankments, borders, abutments, soundproof barriers, and
ventilation stacks. A series of typologies were designed to be adaptable
to the different sites and overall route. Based on simple lines, surfaces,
and volumes, these elements become a part of the motorist's mental
repertoire. The highway is no longer a "no man's land"; it has a face
and identity of its own.

The Les Gripons site provides an excellent example of this approach:
its portals, Mont-Terri North and Mont-Russelin South, are inclined to
the same degree as the mountain slope. The valley portals, Mont-Russelin
North and Mont-Terri South, have quite another configuration: their shape
was defined by the underlying tunnel ventilation system.

◀ TERRI SOUTH (LES GRIPONS)
▼ RUSSELIN NORTH (LES GRIPONS)

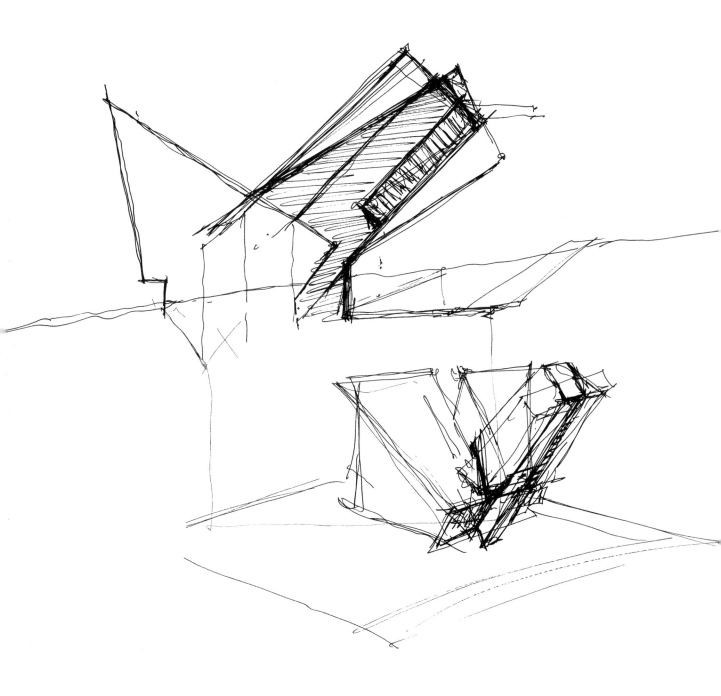

◀ TERRI NORTH VENTILATION STATION
▲ TERRI NORTH SKETCH

BONCOURT-FRANCE

PORRENTRUY WEST

PORRENTRUY EAST

ST-URSANNE

DELÉMONT WEST

Covered trench
of la Beuchille

Balastière upper
passageway

Delémont interchange

DELÉMONT EAST

MOUTIER

SECTIONS 1-2

SECTION 3

SECTIONS 4-5-6

SECTION 7

SECTION 8

A context-based response

In theory, the idea was to develop a standard design for the ventilation, as well as for the portals, upper passageways, abutments, soundproof barriers, etc. In practice, different solutions had to be found for each location and for several reasons including the complexity of the elements, the varying topographical settings, methods of execution specific to each construction company, and implementation periods that spanned several years. However, these individual pockets of vocabulary developed a common thread, which ultimately unifies all of the works. For instance, the lower passageway at the Balastière echoes the forward incline of the front lateral walls, while the middle wall was geometrically inversed to emphasize the opening created by two traffic lanes. The curved contour of the Beuchille gallery portal shows that the structure was not drilled into the mountainside, but rather carved out of it.

◄ ▼ LA BALASTIERE UPPER PASSAGEWAY

BONCOURT-FRANCE

PORRENTRUY WEST

PORRENTRUY EAST

ST-URSANNE

DELÉMONT WEST

DELÉMONT EAST
Choindez North portal
Choindez South portal
Roche St-Jean portal
Bridge over
la Birse (RC6)

MOUTIER

SECTIONS 1-2

SECTION 3

SECTIONS 4-5-6

SECTION 7

SECTION 8

Scale

Scale was fundamental for all of the civil engineering works. It is what enabled each structure to be seen in relation to both its immediate and distant context in a dual reading: from within the infrastructure for the motorist, and from outside of it for the pedestrian.

With its base sitting in the Birse waterway, the St-Jean portal is set in a magnificent landscape, more mineral than vegetal. The occasional tree dramatically punctuates the gorge's crests, evoking Japanese landscape prints.

The crag's vertical flank is an integral element in the project and wraps around the structure. Entirely made of concrete, the portal stands out from the mountainside due to its geometric precision and smooth, poured facades. The awning is designed to protect it from falling rocks, while its lateral wall guards against possible landslides. The portal's abutments and joints, as well as the embankment, are all carefully harmonized to give this site a unifying identify. The construction of the Choindez South portal, directly in front, is currently underway.

◀ ▼ LA ROCHE ST-JEAN PORTAL

▲ LA BIRSE BRIDGE (RC6)
◀ LA ROCHE ST-JEAN PORTAL

Architecture

In 2008, Renato Salvi was invited to speak at the Lausanne Architectural Forum.[1] This was an opportunity to present an architecture studio that had just hit the ten-year mark and conference participants may have expected to leave that evening with a general overview of his projects. But the title of the presentation set an unexpected tone from the start: "Patiently gather, glean and reap certain everyday emotions in order to set out for the imaginary."[2] Renato Salvi surprised the audience with what could be called an "at the source" reading of his work: rather than project a series of images of buildings by his studio, he chose to reveal his process and his references.

I mention this conference because it provides a fundamental key to understanding Renato Salvi's work: with no preconceptions and a strong curiosity, he brings to his projects a vision made up of multiple references.

Rather than impose a singular point of view, Renato Salvi creates a form of architecture that enters into dialogue with a particular context, with the site's history, as well as with his own travel references, focusing on certain elements that may at first seem insignificant.

Beyond the choice of materiality or form, it is this need for multiple anchoring points that constitutes one of the fundamental aspects of Renato Salvi's architectural production.

In Dialogue with Context

"I strongly believe in the idea that disrupting what is given can have vaster repercussions."[3]
Renato Salvi

———

The first type of anchoring point relates to an attitude toward context and landscape that is particularly evident in several villas created since 2000.

Built in 2000 in the hills of Delémont, the Paumier Villa is the first in this series. This brick stucco construction is built on two floors with a partial basement, and sits on a gentle slope offering a nice view of the valley. The project was designed as an intersection

NICOL FURNITURE STORE,
PORRENTRUY, JURA (CH)

of two rectangles. It allows for a vast diagonal panorama and, despite relatively modest metric dimensions, gives the impression of a generous space. An emphasis was placed on the topographical details of the location: the villa was placed carefully on the plot so as to avoid any unnecessary movement of land during construction. This illustrates a main concern for Renato Salvi: things have a reason for being and anything added to a context must be linked to what already exists. An attitude illustrated by the low wall of the terrace that extends laterally from the south facade, creating a strong connection with the surrounding area. Despite its apparent fragility, this wall becomes a fundamental element that allows the villa to clearly affirm its presence on the site.

▲ MAITRE VILLA,
SAIGNELEGIER, JURA (CH)

For the Maître Villa built in Saignelégier in 2004, Renato Salvi uses what we could call spatial micro-geography as a theme for setting down the building. Built in exposed concrete, the house is based on a rectangular plan and on a single level (with the exception of a partial basement area). Only the terrace and its cantilever emerge from the volume. Unlike other villas, and thanks to a lack of any neighboring constructions, Renato Salvi was able to generously open the living spaces to the surrounding area through large bay windows. Set at the edge of a forest on the one side, and facing the magnificent Franches-Montagnes plateau on the other, the particularities of the plot were given heightened importance. Running from the main street to the front door, the pathway becomes a pretext for discovering the geology and vegetation that are characteristic of this region, a theme that extends into the villa. Rocks found outside during construction were left as is, and have become a picturesque backdrop when seen through the large bay windows of the dining room and main bathroom.

For the Montavon Villa in Porrentruy, a whole other strategy toward site elements was put into place. While the main house plan is also rectangular in shape, the actual footprint of the house is reduced thanks to an exposed prestressed concrete structure that creates a series of cantilevers on either side of the villa. Considering the location of the house – that of a typical villa neighborhood with close proximity to its neighbors – Renato Salvi chose an approach that bypassed the direct relationship with the surrounding area: he brought the landscape from afar and made it "enter" the interior spaces, so to speak. The southern two-story extremity is suspended and completely open to the distant landscape, producing a certain effect of detachment from the immediate local environment (both factual and figurative), and as a result, a sense of privacy. To take full advantage of this view and particularly for the dining room, located street side, Renato Salvi introduced a patio on the first floor. This outdoor room, dug out of the overall volume, creates a connection between all the spaces across the length of the villa. But the true strength of this element is that it introduces a particular play on perceptions into the very heart of the dwelling: through the transparency of windows, the landscape is reflected into the house, creating a sense of indivisibility between the valley and the villa itself.

The Ruedin Villa also uses a distant landscape as a the key element of the design, but this time nature plays a dominant and direct role in shaping the exterior form – and specifically the slope of the roof. Viewed from the back, the slope of the villa's roof mimics the angle of the mountain crest located on the other side of the Rhône plain, like a visual echo. These two elements, architecture and nature, are linked to the scale of the valley and become part of one and the same landscape.

▲ RUEDIN VILLA,
AYENT, VALAIS (CH)

Travel References

"When one travels and works with visual things — architecture, painting or sculpture- one uses one's eyes and draws, so as to fix deep in one's experience what is seen."[4]
Le Corbusier

The relationship to spatial context can sometimes be enriched by references gathered from travels. Creatively reinterpreted, they give certain projects an anchoring point in a different realm, as can be seen in the following four examples.

The first example is that of the Bastardoz Villa built in Cheyres in 2005. The plan is quite simple, based on a rectangular form. In order to benefit from the magnificent view of the Neuchâtel Lake and its surrounding vineyards, however, the sections were developed over three floors. The main area, consisting of the living area, dining room and terrace, is located on the third floor. While the house acts as a retaining wall, set against a steeply inclined terrain, a three-story high open space appears at the entrance to the building to create a sense of unity between the three levels. This space is a direct reference to a house built in the 1930s, now abandoned and practically in ruins that Renato Salvi discovered in the Bologna countryside. Fascinated by the way in which nature had invited itself into the building through openings in the walls and roof, Renato Salvi photographed this space on several occasions and used it as a model to connect the Bastardoz Villa to its surrounding natural elements. When one passes the portico that leads to the front entrance of the house, the forest that sits to the back of the parcel is immediately visible – and is invited, in a sense, into the villa itself. Once again, as was the case with the Paumier Villa, there is a connection to the surrounding area at the extremity of the building. But this time it is done by creating an empty space: the architect does not add an element to lengthen the construction, but rather carves out and literally dematerializes one side of the building — perhaps unconsciously looking for the same state of ruin that he found in the Italian countryside.

▲ R. SALVI, A 1930s VILLA
IN RUIN, BOLOGNE,
PHOTOGRAPH
▲ BASTARDOZ VILLA ,
CHEYRES , FRIBOURG
(CH)

Just above the Bastardoz Villa and also in Cheyres, a hillside villa presents a much more organic shape due to a disjuncture in volume, both in the plan and the cross sections, yielding a very rich sense of interior space. What comes to mind here is the

▼ R. SALVI, COTTAGE, SICILY, PHOTOGRAPH
▼ HILLSIDE VILLA IN CHEYRES, FRIBOURG (CH)
▼ R. SALVI, BRION CEMETERY, SCARPA, PHOTOGRAPH
▼ SCHALLER VILLA, REBEUVELIER, JURA (CH)

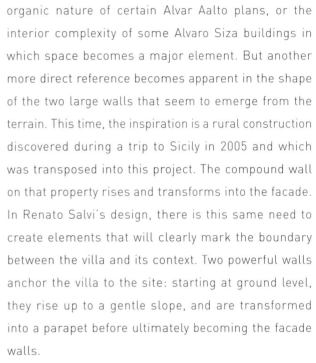

organic nature of certain Alvar Aalto plans, or the interior complexity of some Alvaro Siza buildings in which space becomes a major element. But another more direct reference becomes apparent in the shape of the two large walls that seem to emerge from the terrain. This time, the inspiration is a rural construction discovered during a trip to Sicily in 2005 and which was transposed into this project. The compound wall on that property rises and transforms into the facade. In Renato Salvi's design, there is this same need to create elements that will clearly mark the boundary between the villa and its context. Two powerful walls anchor the villa to the site: starting at ground level, they rise up to a gentle slope, and are transformed into a parapet before ultimately becoming the facade walls.

Also worth mentioning is the Schaller Villa, completed in 2003 in Rebeuvelier and located on the border between the village and an agricultural zone. The parcel of land ends right where the cultivated fields begin, and Renato Salvi chose the height of the wheat stalks before harvest as the altimetric benchmark for the villa. Here, the reference is to the Brion cemetery, a project by Italian architect Carlo Scarpa in which the height of the surrounding wheat stalks defines the height of the enclosure wall. But this time, the reference is less literal than in the previous example: here, Renato Salvi inverses the relationship between nature and architecture. The Scarpa project uses the wheat stalks as a way to crown the surrounding wall. The Schaller Villa, however, seems to float above the height of the stalks, sitting on a vegetal carpet of sorts and giving the construction a sense of fragility and lightness.

In the extension project for a training school located at Porrentruy, Renato Salvi engaged with a context that involved a series of constructions built at different stages since the 1980s and with no clear sense of hierarchy between them. By designing his construction as an extension to the main building, he provided the complex with a centerpiece: half the volume of his building extension juts out as a cantilever to create a covered courtyard. Because of their physicality and perpendicular orientation, the powerful lateral walls could have been perceived as disjointed from the existing building. To avoid this, Renato Salvi designed an artificial addition to the old building, thus creating a link between the two structures. Another Roman building probably inspired this approach: the Girasole by architect Luigi Moretti. Not having found any ruins in the construction of his building (which is usually the case in Rome!) the disappointed architect decided to draw fake ruins into his project as a base for the new building. This gave him the freedom to create on his own the very condition he was looking for. Renato Salvi remembered this project and proceeded in a similar manner: on the facade of the existing building, he added a concrete volume similar in form to that of the lateral walls (the new secondary entrance) that stretches out to the new extension via a long bench, also in concrete. Thanks to an intervention that did not exist before, a new link was created between the two heterogeneous elements on this site.

▼ PORRENTRUY VOCATIONAL
TRAINING CENTER, JURA (CH)

Memory of a Space

————

"History as a light source." Renato Salvi.

There is one last type of anchoring point that is inherent in a range of projects by Renato Salvi, from public buildings to renovations: the memory of a space.

The Delémont train station will be the first major urban renovation for his architecture studio. Won by competition in 2000, it will offer the opportunity to reflect on a very important interface: that of a train station, the point of entry into a town.

The first part of the process was to get rid of all the additions made to the building over the course of time, giving it back its original figure. Only the entrances were redesigned in a more contemporary idiom. Tearing down the old cloakroom allowed for the creation of a long building that will house various businesses, linked to the old building by an awning. The positioning of the new building, on plan, is very precise: it respects the width of the demolished building. Between these two interventions, the architect places the access to the underground passageway, which becomes the centerpiece of the complex: this is where the old and the new will coexist in the most powerful manner. Where in the past one went down a modest staircase to reach the platforms, we are now guided by a two-story space that presents a series of stairways leading to the different areas of the station. Made of exposed concrete, this space slips under what is a typical Swiss train station awning made of stained wood and painted metal, thus complementing the old structure but with a contemporary use of material.

The intervention is intended as a simple one, requiring a modest financial outlay, but allowing for a sense of unity by combining the newer elements with the old.

In the renovation of the Porrentruy state school, we can also see this desire to use "history as a source of light" for the present, as a way to feed the imagination and guide an intervention strategy. Here, the idea of an old seminary is revealed, notably in the access hallways along which the new classroom additions will be built. The existing windows, sunk into thick stone walls, become niches where students can study. Across the hall, Renato Salvi chooses to place a series of wooden panels directly in front of these niches, housing the hallway lighting system, but also serving as access doors to the new classrooms. The nature of this space, designed for studies, is to a certain extent materialized by elements that draw the visitor into an almost monastic universe, reminiscent of the cell doors that can be found in certain convents. Located at the other end of the building, the old chapel was simply renovated to accentuate this particular atmosphere. Between the two spaces, the architect uses a contemporary style for the elevator and staircases, which blends well with the material presence of the past.

In the renovation of a sixteenth century building in Delémont's old town, and for himself this time, Renato Salvi — without transforming the building in its entirety — only affected the space in certain areas, keeping a certain "respect toward the ancestors." At a careful distance, he was able to introduce three elements without disturbing the past or any traces left by past inhabitants. To meet the present needs of the building occupants, only a stairway, a kitchen and a passage to an outside gallery area were added. The rest of the building was simply restored.

A different attitude was adopted for the Kaufman cottage renovation in the village of Rocourt. The inside of this building had already undergone a series of successive renovations, and had been left in very bad shape, therefore removing the possibility of preserving any pre-existing element. In order for the new renovation to recreate a link with the memory of this site, the interior spaces of the old cottage were entirely emptied and rebuilt, but with care taken to introduce a dimensional system using the same proportions as the old inner spaces. In this way, the typology met the needs of the new owners – notably in the creation of an open-space kitchen and living area on the ground level – while the general atmosphere still reminded the inhabitants that they were living in an old cottage, thanks to the height of the ceilings most notably, and despite the contemporary materials and the new extension to the plan.

One of the more recent renovations by his studio is also in Porrentruy: the Nicol furniture store. The challenge was to renovate a building in the old town that had been entirely rebuilt in the 1980s. At that time, the architect had chosen to use an "old-fashioned" style, including roofs of differing inclinations overhanging discontinuous volumes. To be rid of these historic illusions, Renato Salvi kept the exterior volume, which was the most representative element of the building, but covered the entire building with a radical intervention: an envelope of vertical wooden strips. The exterior form therefore became paramount, both in its relation to the surrounding buildings and by reaffirming its affiliation to the whole, without denying a

▲ GARDEN OF THE NICOL FURNI-
TURE STORE, PORRENTRUY,
JURA (CH)

certain distinctness. A play on perception was set in place in which the "fake old-fashioned" aspect of the building was hidden in the background and only revealed depending on the visitor's position. Once inside, a few specific renovations were made to create a link to certain elements of the site, such as the back garden that was completely abandoned during the reconstruction. A facade wall was sawn and simply toppled over onto the ground, becoming a terrace and creating a link to the chateau located in the back area. Thus, a connection was re-established and a certain historic honesty was restored.

In going through a few of Renato Salvi's projects, I have tried to provide a guide to the better deciphering of his works through the introduction of a relevant theme, that of anchoring points. We then saw how this theme was applied in different ways, whether relating to anchoring work to a context, to travel references, or to the memory of a space.

Impressions and images gleaned during a journey, in reading a book or in the presence of a landscape come feed the imagination and reveal themselves in different forms in Renato Salvi's projects. But what is of particular interest is that the architect, in taking this approach, mixes together resources drawn from different, and sometimes disjointed contexts or eras. By placing them in relation to each other, he plays on the notion of geographical, cultural and historic frontiers and creates altogether new connections.

Renato Salvi is an architect whose attitude is fundamentally cultural in the sense that he is able to create links beyond the boundaries of the project itself, be they physical or psychological. This is how Renato Salvi's work speaks to us, in this very capacity to bring together different resources in order to better ground his projects, all the while projecting them out to another, vaster totality.

1. *Carte blanche 5*, Forum d'architecture, April 10, 2008.
2. Translated from the French, "Glaner, grapiller, récolter patiemment certaines émotions dans son quotidien pour se mettre en route vers son imaginaire."
3. Translated from the French, "Je crois profondément à l'idée que de bouleverser ce qui nous est donné se répercute de façon plus vaste."
4. Le Corbusier, *Creation is a Patient Search*, trans. James Palmes (New York: Frederick A. Praeger, 1960), p. 37.

The training center is the third consecutive construction in a series of buildings built between 1970 and 1980. The extension became the centerpiece of the complex through a prominent cantilever that serves as a covered courtyard area. The three buildings in this complex are harmonized through a specific approach to the exterior spaces: large concrete slabs on the ground and a new entrance attached to the older buildings follow the same vanishing point as the bottom area of the new extension. Understanding this project requires taking into account these unifying factors.

The hallways are first and foremost considered as meeting areas. The classrooms, with floor-to-ceiling windows, face the surrounding countryside, while some rooms have translucent glass walls to reduce the sensation of lateral division.

In its combination of basic elements – walls, glazing, doors – the building does not seek to be technologically innovative, but rather to conjure serenity and poetic harmony.

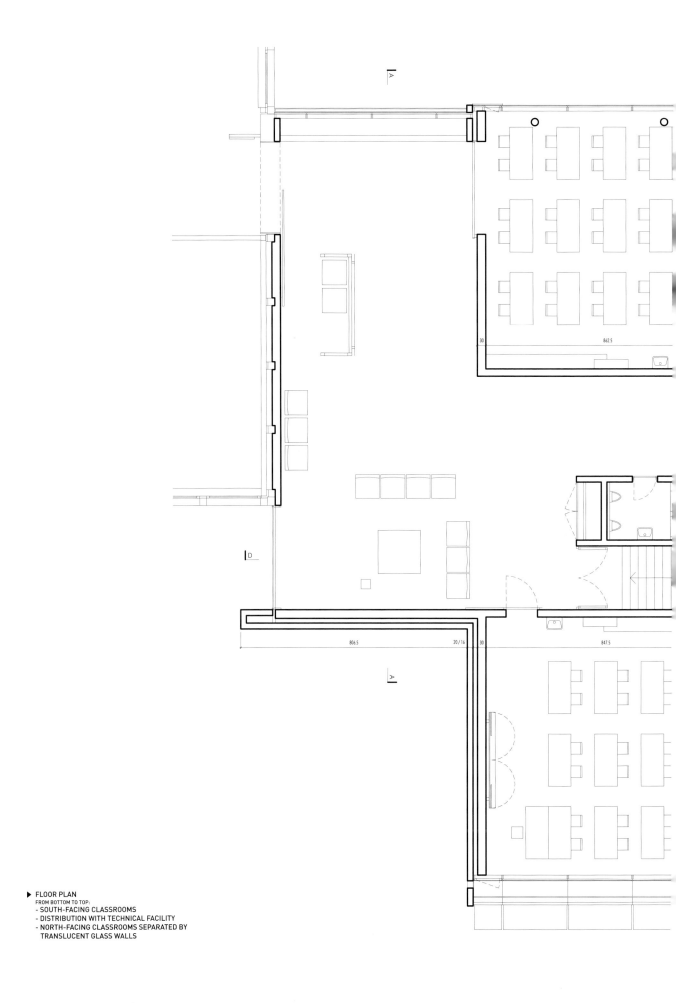

▶ FLOOR PLAN
FROM BOTTOM TO TOP:
- SOUTH-FACING CLASSROOMS
- DISTRIBUTION WITH TECHNICAL FACILITY
- NORTH-FACING CLASSROOMS SEPARATED BY
  TRANSLUCENT GLASS WALLS

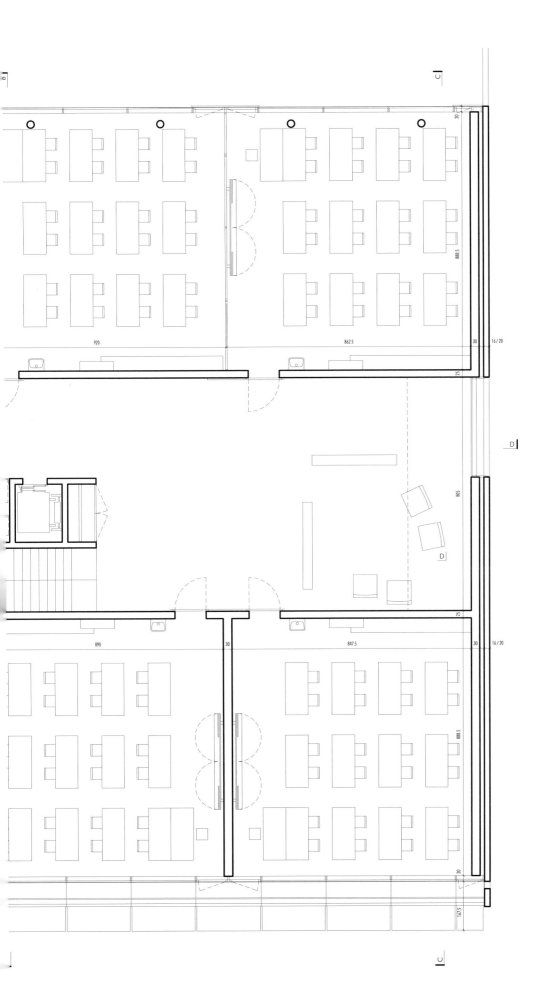

How should an architect approach an imposing seventeenth-century Jura heritage building? What is the building's history and how were its successive renovations and adaptations fashioned over time? How can new technical and energy standards be met without distorting the building's original character? On the one hand, the project was uncompromising in its emphasis on a contemporary style of renovation. On the other hand, it included a series of precise studies that sought to reinterpret the existing repetitive building elements, which include doors, windows, light fixtures, and moldings.

Once a seminary, then an elementary school, and today a state secondary school, the building's original austere and studious character has been preserved and restored, along with the constructed substance or identity of the building.

The existing building speaks for itself, and all external spaces — as well as the way in which they are lit at night — serve to reinforce its natural presence. As with any act of creation, any modification is a deed culturally representative of its era.

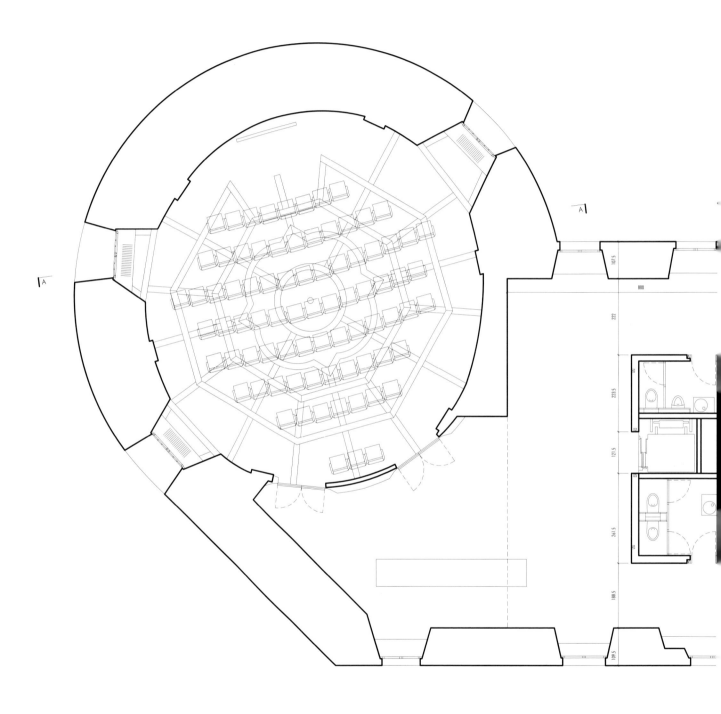

▶ FLOOR PLAN
FROM LEFT TO RIGHT:
- CHAPEL
- NEW TECHNICAL FACILITY
- CLASSROOMS

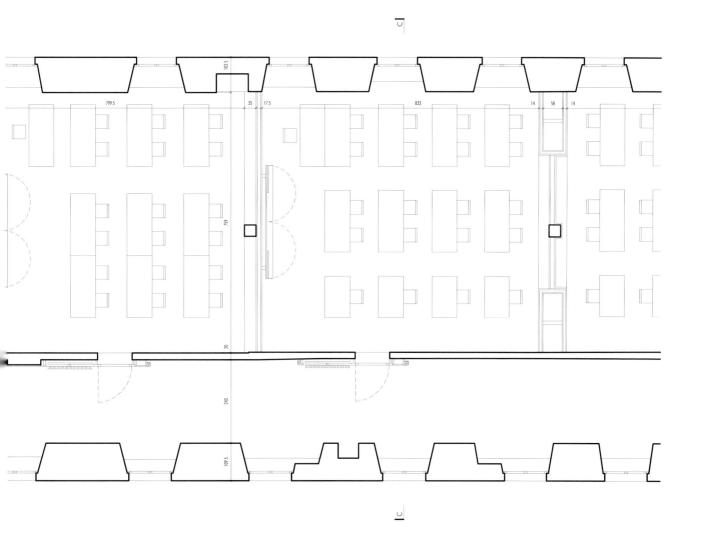

The train station is a portal onto other spaces, a place for meetings and exchanges. For this contemporary renovation, it was important to choose a layout that would be appropriate to the scale of the city of Delémont. The different elements making up the train station – original buildings, underground passageways, access ramps, the commercial strip, and central square – were each designed in relation to each other, to infuse the site with a new urban vitality. With great regard for restoration, the original building has regained its initial perimeter following the demolition of annexes that had been added over time. Original bricked-up window frames have thus been uncovered and restored.

Designed primarily in concrete and dropping under the old wooden awning, the access area under the rails has been widened and leads to a two-story space. The footbridge between the two platforms has been sectioned and moved to the pedestrian side of the ramp to allow for maximum brightness and sunlight into the underground passage. The bicycle park marks the platform boundary and, on the track side, provides a covered seating area.

An awning of about a hundred meters links the old building to a new retail center. Night lighting accentuates the awning and makes it an active part of community life.

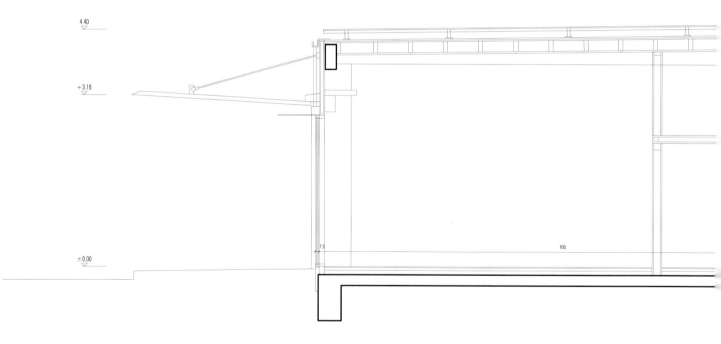

4.40

+ 3.18

± 0.00

7.5   930

▶ TRANSVERSAL SECTION
FROM LEFT TO RIGHT:
- AWNING
- RETAIL CENTER
- BICYCLE PARK
- TRACK

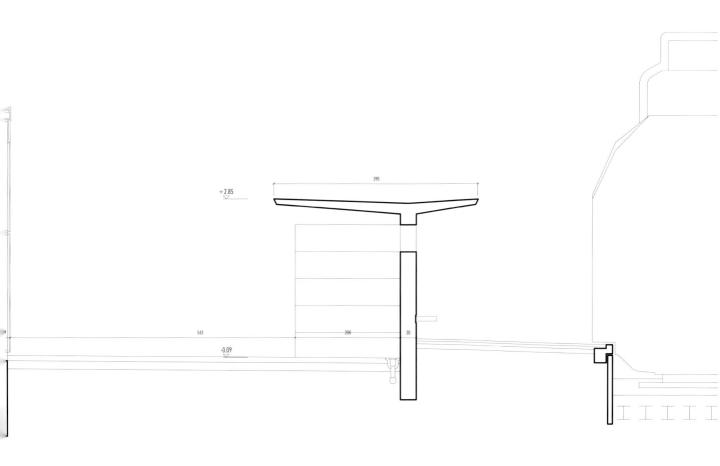

+ 2.85

390

543

-0.09

200   30

Bastardoz Villa in Cheyres

To the north, a view of the Lake of Neuchâtel; to the south, the hillside and forest. The terrain's incline and narrow boundaries determined both the building's alignment and its embrace of the plot's various curves and levels. It also led to the construction of terraces at each end of the building, thus creating surprising exterior spaces, whilst providing a large open-air hall area at the entrance. To the south, the glass roof lets in light and establishes a strong visual relationship with the forest. The aerial and fluid living room on the top floor seems to be suspended between earth and sky. In keeping with this notion, the actual structure – designed in collaboration with the engineer Laurent Chablais – is integrated into the window frames in the form of poles and beams, thus making it practically invisible.

An eggplant color is used for the exterior of the villa — in contrast to the white interior spaces — allowing it to melt into the luxuriant surrounding countryside.

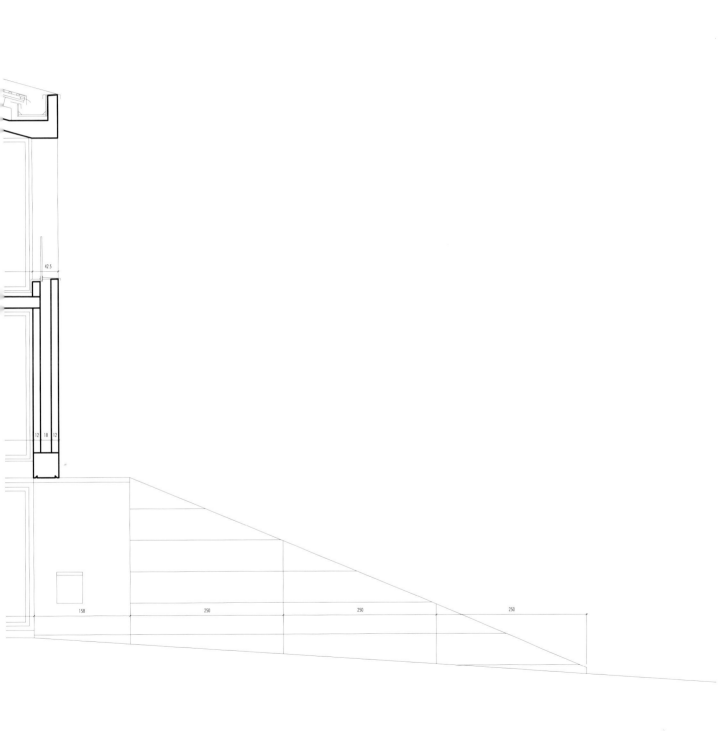

42.5

12 18 12

158   250   250   250

The house is located on a steep hill above Porrentruy. Given its setting in a residential neighborhood, a relationship to the distant landscape is favored. Organized over three levels and made entirely of concrete, it resembles a fortress in style. The house occupies very little ground space, given a very difficult topographical situation. Built as an exterior space and extension to the kitchen, the patio is a room open to the sky and landscape, but screened from view, as well as from sun and wind. The two-story living area benefits not only from the southern light shining through the large bay windows, but also from a northwest light coming in from the patio area above.

The partially sunk, second space is located under the south cantilever and generously opens out into the distance. Adjacent to the swimming pool, it is a space for relaxing and provides shade in the summer months. The prestressed cantilever at the entrance is balanced with the living area's cantilever. The former serves to guide toward and protect the entrance, while the latter projects the inhabitants out into the landscape, thus making the neighboring villas appear to recede.

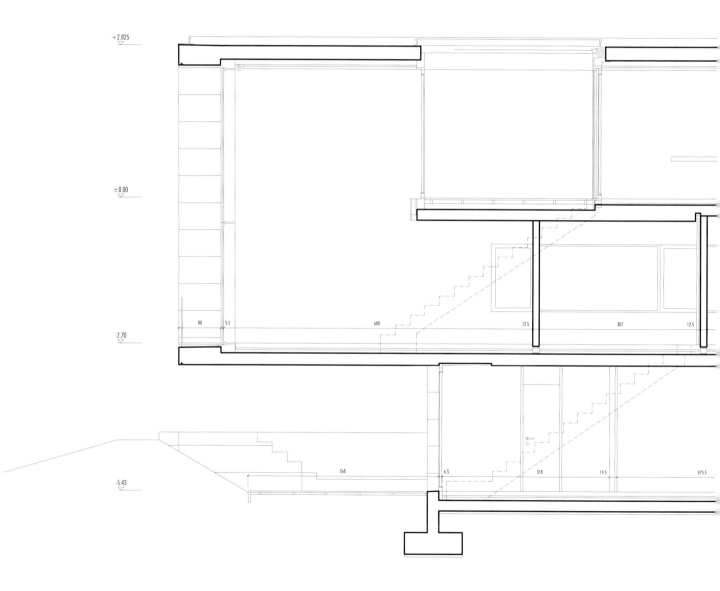

+ 2.825

± 0.00

-2.70

-5.43

80   5.5   600   12.5   307   12.5

368   6.5   318   14.5   475.5

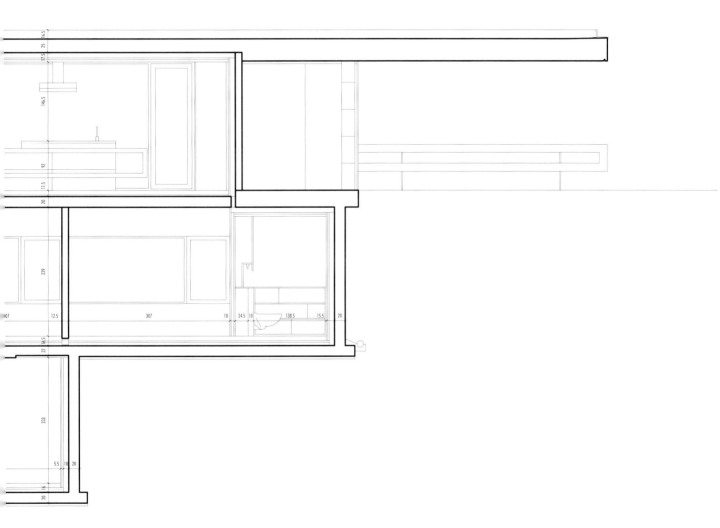

◀ LONGITUDINAL SECTION
FROM RIGHT TO LEFT:
- GARAGE
- DINING ROOM AND KITCHEN
- PATIO
- LIVING ROOM
- BALCONY

At the edge of the forest and on a magnificent but steeply inclined plot, the villa is set on a base – a traditional technique that allows it to be detached from the land and thus reveals the exact topography of the location. The villa has no garden and the surrounding fields, left intact, provide the backdrop.

The house is hardly visible from the top. At the back, it opens out onto a micro-landscape of protruding rocks and a dry-stone wall that separates it from the forest. To the south, however, large bay windows offer a direct relationship to the distant landscape. The large cantilever terrace extends outward to this very landscape, seeking an even more intense communion. Unlike the sleeping areas, the day rooms enjoy a double ceiling.

Access to the villa is progressive: to get from the road, located at a higher level, to the villa below, the visitor must use elements that evolve over the course of the walk: a simple concrete band on the ground transforms first into walls, then into a staircase, and finally becomes the entrance awning, thus creating a gentle progression between the public and private realms.

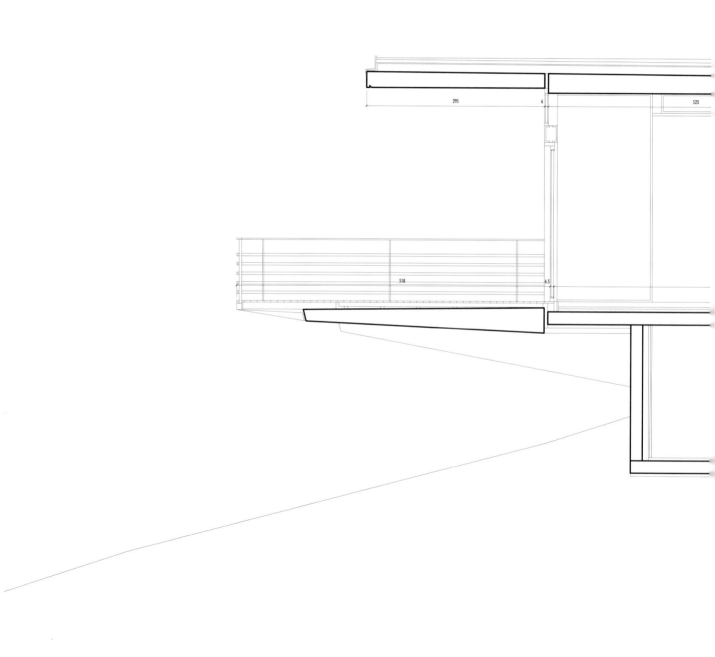

295   6   523

518   6.5

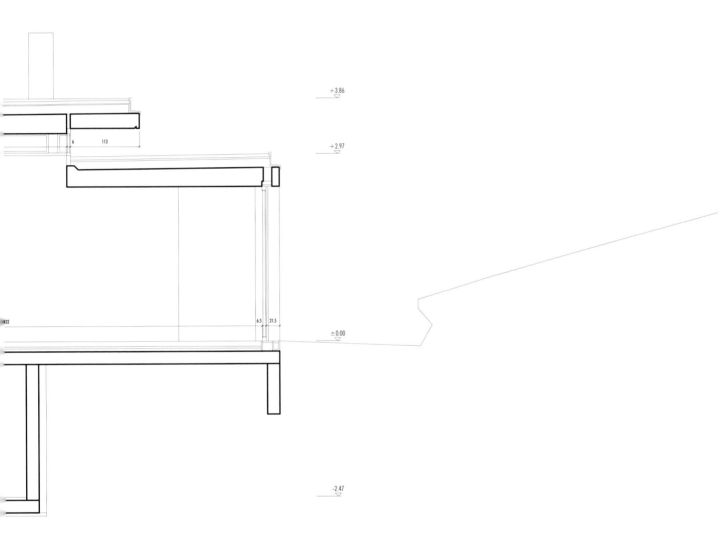

+ 3.86

6   113

+ 2.97

K32

6.5   21.5

± 0.00

-2.47

◀ CROSS SECTION
FROM LEFT TO RIGHT:
- TERRACE
- LIVING ROOM
- BACK GARDEN

A series of non-orthogonal walls create an interior space that cascades in different directions. The walls shape the area on every side and allow for the interior spaces to box successively into each other. On the top floor, the entrance has no direct view to the exterior: light enters evocatively through the bottom of a bay window in the living area in an inversed and unusual relationship, creating a surprising effect and a fleeting emotion.

The awning that extends over the entire length of the villa is highly unusual for this type of project, enriching the house by giving it a new scale and particular strength. The A16 highway experience was undoubtedly significant here: as with the highway, an economy in terms of forms of expression was sought after for the house, even if this may not be immediately obvious.

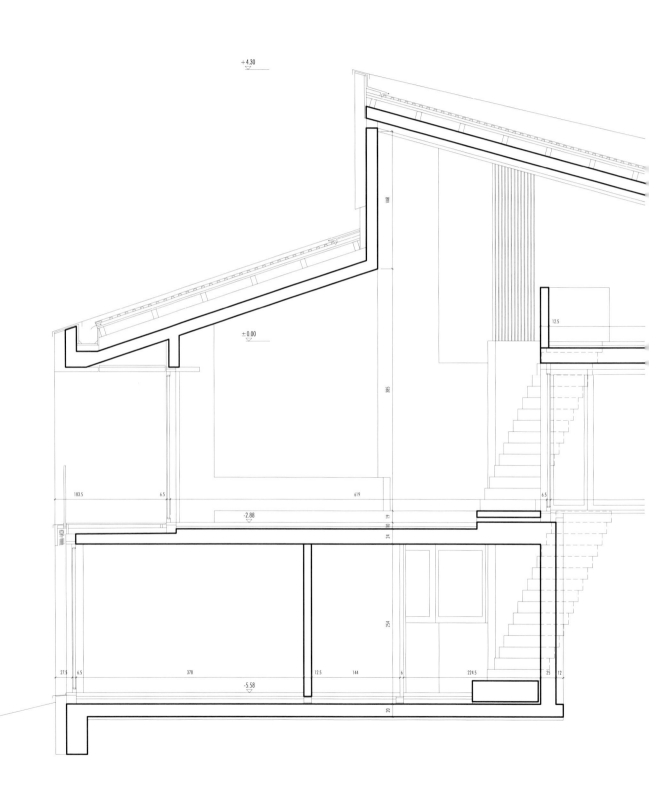

+4.30

±0.00

VAR

385

183.5   6.5   619

-2.88

10 19

24

254

27.5 6.5   378   12.5   144   6   224.5   25 12

-5.58

20

12.5

6.5

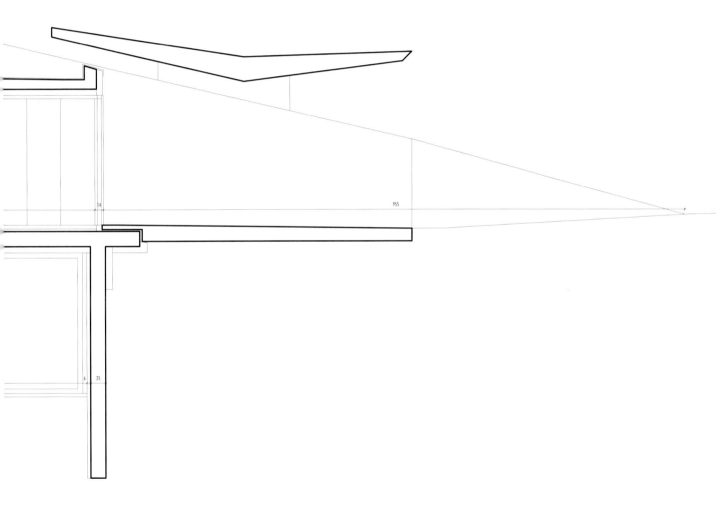

34

955

6   25

◄ CROSS SECTION
FROM RIGHT TO LEFT:
- GARAGE
- ENTRANCE
- LIVING ROOM
- TERRACE

The house is located on the hillside, at the edge of the vineyards, and at an inflection point. The view is extraordinary, both to the south and to the north. Set in parallel to the topographic lines, the house stretches lengthwise to receive maximum sunlight. A large single-sloped roof partially covers the house, encompassing bedrooms and working areas on the first floor. The children's rooms to the west, at ground level, are entirely independent. A dug-out patio is wholly integrated into the volumetric analysis and is protected from view, as well as from the southern sun and wind. The adjoining kitchen directly faces the landscape.

The roof's incline was found to be aligned to the distant mountain slope. The fact that this was unintentional makes it all the more fascinating.

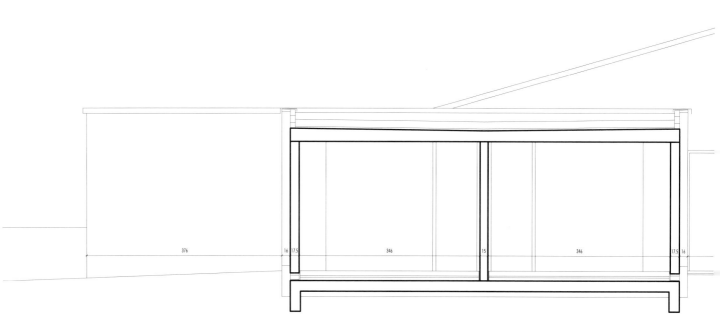

376   16 17.5   346   15 17.5   346   17.5 16

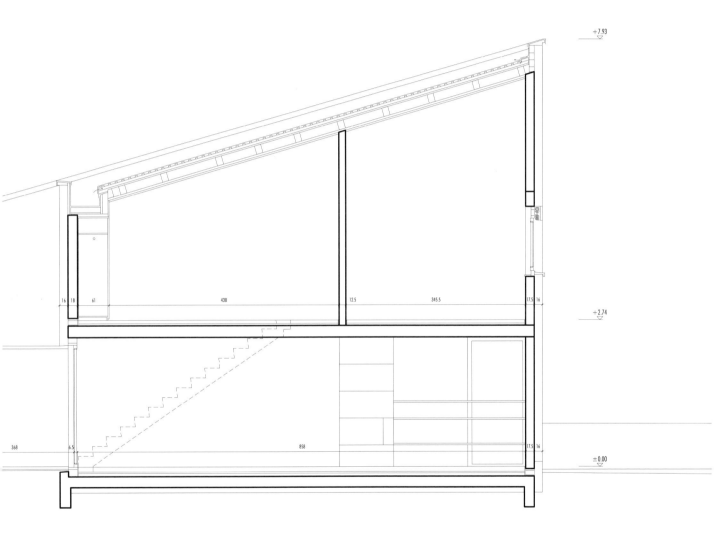

+7.93

16 18   61   438   12.5   345.5   17.5 16   +2.74

368   6.5   858   17.5 16   ± 0.00

◀ LONGITUDINAL SECTION
FROM LEFT TO RIGHT:
- BEDROOMS
- TERRACE
- LIVING ROOM (BOTTOM)
  AND BEDROOMS (TOP)

This house is located in the hills of Delémont at the foot of a nineteenth-century villa. The old gate's two pillars, accentuated by two linden trees, serve as the entrance and also as an anchoring point; bamboos delineate this access area.

While the project favors mostly diagonal lines to open up the space, the cross section is sensitive to the terrain's slight incline, further emphasized by both the exterior and interior stepped walkways. The constructed elements of the villa are simple and standard, but it is altogether very sculptural in its exterior form. The volume proportions, the relationship between open and closed spaces, the typology of its doors and windows — and so the quality of the indoor light — have shaped, sketched, chiseled this space.

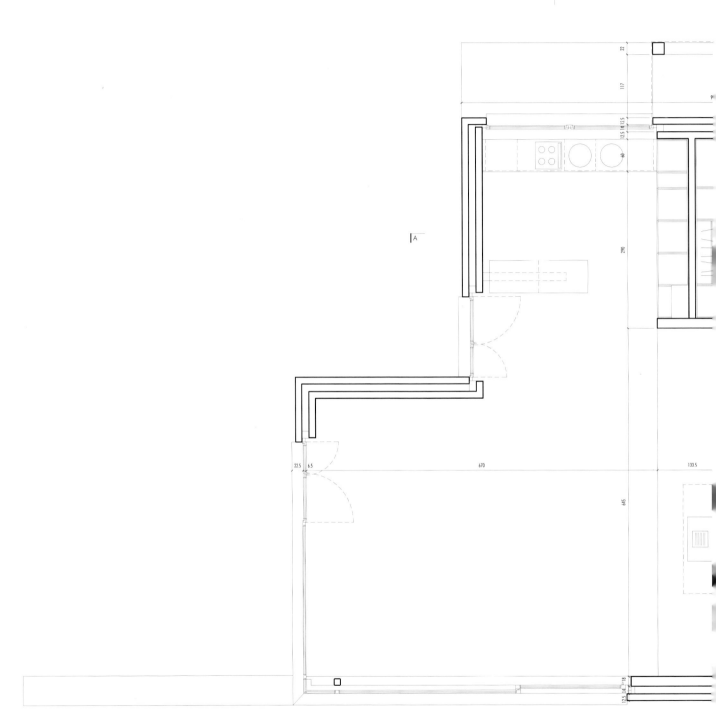

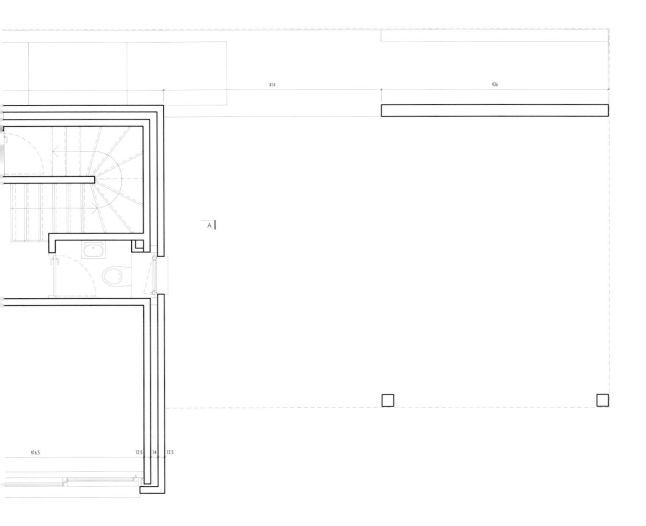

414   436

A

416.5   12.5 14 12.5

◀ GROUND-LEVEL PLAN
FROM RIGHT TO LEFT:
- GARAGE
- ENTRANCE AND GUEST ROOM
- LIVING ROOM AND DINING ROOM / KITCHEN
- TERRACE

A wonderful old orchard is hidden well out of sight behind this farm. Once strictly functional, the orchard became the key element of the project — onto which the living area and kitchen open, toward which dreams will escape.

In very poor shape, the living areas and all successive additions were completely demolished. This total reconstruction sought to recover the atmosphere created by the shadows, half-light, and silence that had previously filled this space.

The village-facing facade was conserved and flowerbeds identical to those found on other farms of the region were replanted.

Nothing was evacuated during the demolition. The old cinder-block walls were made into exterior flooring, benches were fashioned into low walls, old floorboards into vertical cladding across the facade, and the old beams into floor beams.

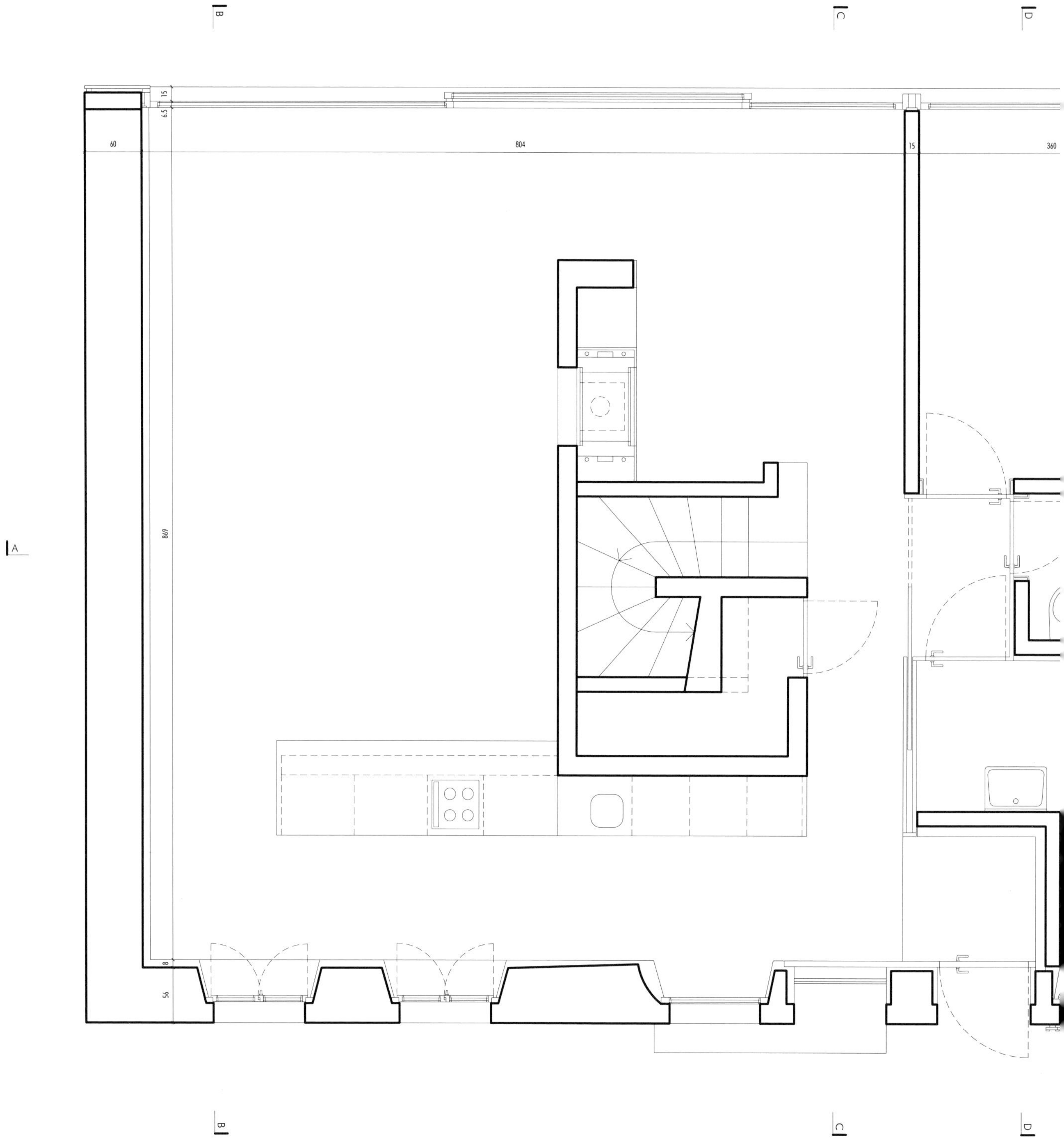

B
C
D
A
15
6.5
60
804
15
360
869
8
56
B
C
D

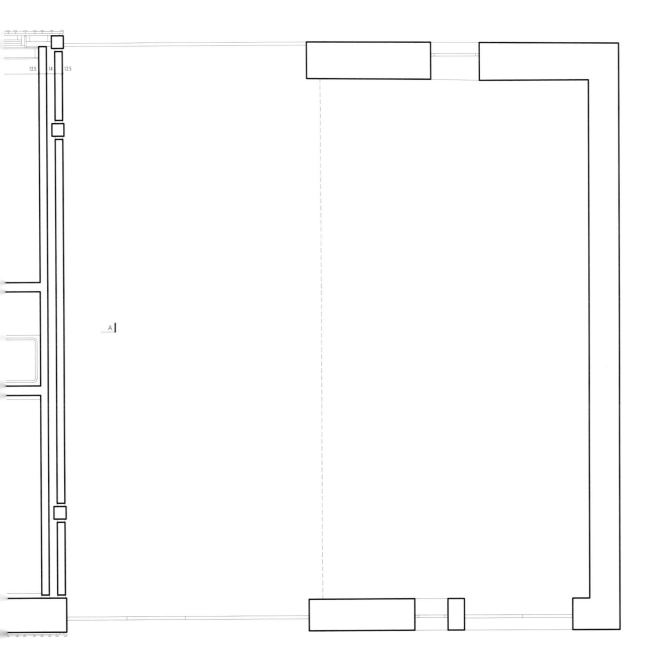

12.5   14   12.5

A

▲ GROUND-LEVEL PLAN
FROM LEFT TO RIGHT:
- LIVING ROOM, DINING ROOM, AND KITCHEN
- CENTRAL FACILITY
- BEDROOM AND LAUNDRY ROOM
- BARN (NOT RENOVATED)

You can never truly own a sixteenth-century edifice. Instead you are its guardian, accompanying it through a particular stretch of time, prolonging its existence, enabling it to reach the next generation. No heavy renovations; rather, constant attention must be paid not to "hurt" the building, not to alter its nature or abuse it in any way. The building itself established how the internal stairway should be introduced, as well as the shape of the kitchen, the opening onto the landing area, and even the materials and colors to be used. The austere atmosphere resulting from the strict plan was faithfully maintained, as were all of the building's constructed substances. The challenge was in being attentive to the past. Sensory experiences was not simply invented but resulted instead from traces left by the passage of time and previous occupants.

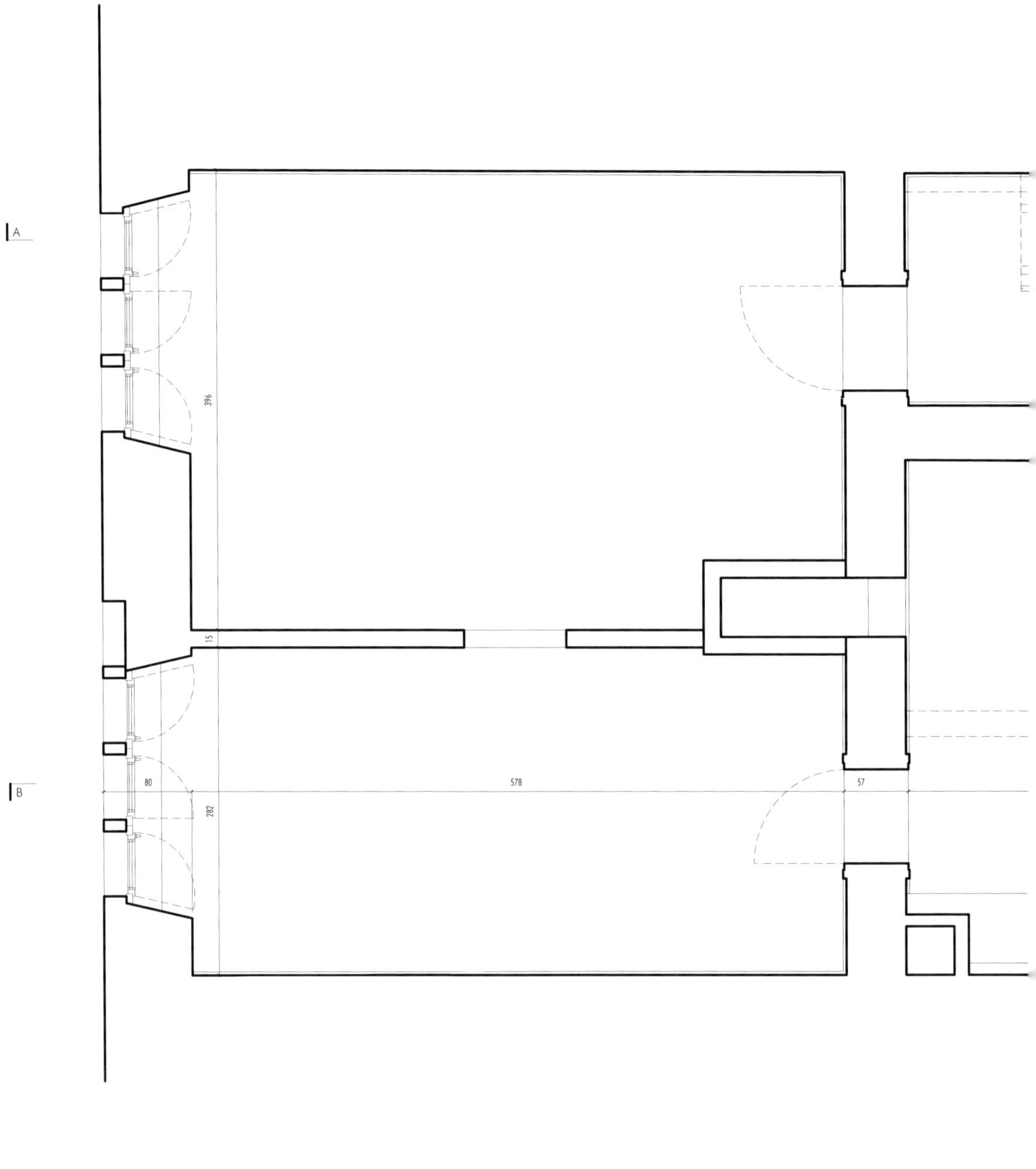

A

396

B

80

282

15

578

57

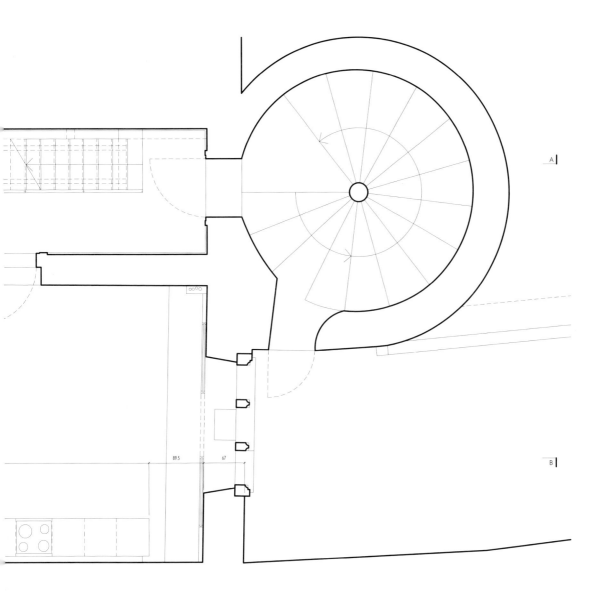

89.5   67

A|

B|

▲ FLOOR PLAN
FROM LEFT TO RIGHT:
- LIVING ROOM AND DINING ROOM
- KITCHEN
- EXTERIOR GALLERY

RENOVATIONS

Private Spa in Mervelier

Attached to an old manor house, this space combines the elements of water and fire with the pursuits of reading, relaxing, and dining.

While on one side it opens generously onto the garden, the back of the building, which faces the street, has been made private with the planting of a screen of birch trees. The centerpiece of the new building is the entrance portico of the old house. Forming two distinct entities, the swimming area, spa, and sauna are located at the entrance level, while the kitchen, fireplace, and reading area are one level below. Wood becomes the ultimate protagonist of the interior spaces. Latticed on the floor, it bends upward to form radiator covers, then evolves into steps, a bench, and finally into the kitchen furniture. The unifying use of this material lends a sense of benevolence to the whole, as well as the mellowness required of this type of place. No lights were tolerated at ceiling level: nighttime lighting comes primarily from water-basin spotlights, and so shines out through water.

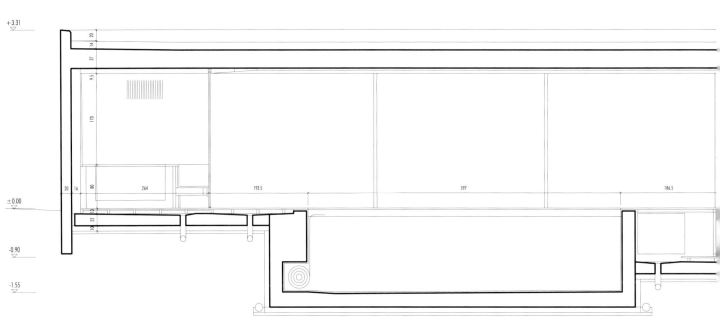

▲ LONGITUDINAL SECTION
FROM LEFT TO RIGHT:
- SPA
- SWIMMING POOL
- LIVING AREA AND KITCHEN
- FIREPLACE
- GARAGE AND TECHNICAL FACILITY

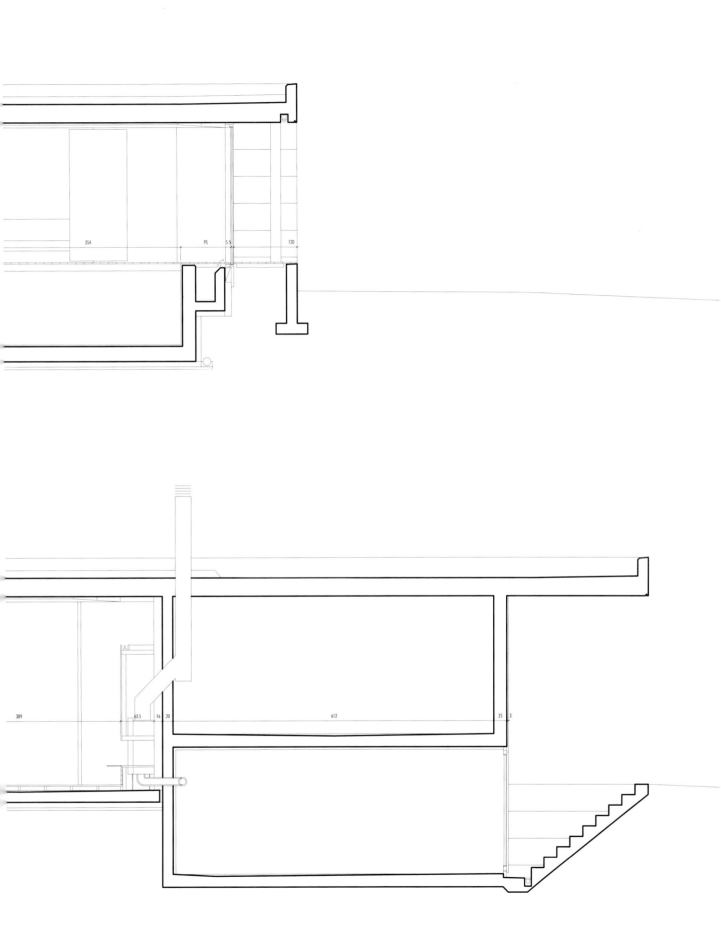

354   95   5.5   120

389   63.5   16   20   612   25   3

Projects
—

> Transjurane A16 highway

Civil engineering structures, Boncourt-France – Porrentruy West (section 2), 2005–2016

- publications (all sections):

Kelly Shannon and Marcel Smets, *The Landscape of Contemporary Infrastructure*, Rotterdam: Nai Publishers, 2010, p. 146.
Domobât, no. 2 (May/June 2008), pp. 26–27.
"Architects Directory 2008," *Wallpaper.com*, http://www.wallpaper.com/directory/883.
Bâtir, no. 12 (December 2007), pp. 16–17.
Architektur erwandern, Zurich: Werd Verlag AG, 2007, pp. 68–75, 153.
"Rencontre avec Renato Salvi, architecte des tunnels de la Transjurane," Télévision Suisse Romande, w/ V. Singh and H. Geney, June 26, 2007.
Défis, no. 16 (May 2007), pp. 12–13.
Tracés, no. 8 (May 9, 2007), pp. 16–20.
Best Architects 07, Düsseldorf: Zinnobergruen GmbH, 2006, pp. 194–97.

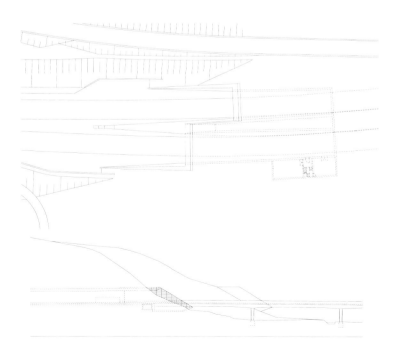

Civil engineering structures, Porrentruy West – Porrentruy East (section 3), 1998–2005

- publications:

Domobât, no. 5 (October/November 2006), pp. 6–8.
Le Cahier de la DRA 2006 (August 2006), p. 26.
L'Hebdo, no. 31 (August 3, 2006), p. 50.
Idea, no. 4 (2006), pp. 24–26.
AS Architecture Suisse, no. 160 (Spring 2006), pp. 35–38.
Domobât, no. 1 (March/April 2006), pp. 58–64.
Plaquette A16 République et Canton du Jura, Evitements de Porrentruy et Delémont (November 2005).
IIC, l'industria italiana del cemento, no. 803 (November 2004), pp. 830–43.
Serena Maffioletti and Stefano Rocchetto, *Infrastrutture e paesaggi contemporanei*, Padua: Il Poligrafo, 2002, pp. 92–95.
Les ouvrages d'art de la Transjurane A16 – Un défi, Delémont: Canton du Jura, 2002.

Civil engineering structures, Porrentruy East – Delémont West (sections 4-5-6)
Communauté de travail la Transjurane (F. Ruchat-Roncati – R. Salvi), 1988–1998

- 1988 competition, 1st price

- publications:

AS Architecture Suisse, no. 146 (September 2002), pp. 23–26.
Bâtir, no. 9 (2001), pp. 20–21.
M. Huber and T. Hildebrand, Switzerland, Ellipsis, London, 2001, pp. 9.2–9.5.
Pierre von Meiss, *Autoroutes et paysages*, Conference notes, EPFL, 2000, pp. 44–49.
Christoph Allenspach, *L'architecture en Suisse*, Zurich: Pro Helvetia, 1999, pp. 156–57.
Martin Heller and Andreas Vogt, ed., *Die Schweizer Autobahn*, exh. cat. Museum Gestaltung Zürich (Zurich, 1999), pp. 252–83.

Civil engineering structures, Delémont West – Delémont East (section 7), 1998–2005

- publications:

Nicolas Faure, *Autoland: Pictures from Switzerland*, exh. cat. Museum Gestaltung Zürich (Zurich, 1999), pp. 95–98.
AMC, le moniteur architecture, no. 97 (April 1999), pp. 68–73.
Architektur & Wohnen Special, no. 6 (April 1999), p. 102.
Architektura & Biznes, no. 7–8 (1999), pp. 17–22.
Roderick Hönig and Benedikt Loderer, *La Romandie existe*, Zurich: Verlag Hochparterre, 1998, pp. 106–7.
Hochparterre, "Die besten '98" supplement, no. 12 (1998), pp. 5–7.
Faces, no. 44 (Summer 1998), p. 1.
Rivista tecnica, no. 4 (1996), pp. 4–15.
Chantiers, no. 4 (1994), pp. 19–25.

Civil engineering structures, Delémont East – Choindez (section 8), 2005–2016

- Architecture prizes:

First prize, Prix d'architecture suisse 1998 (*Hochparterre* and *10 vor 10*), for the A16, in collaboration with Flora Ruchat-Roncati
Nomination, Distinction Romande d'Architecture 2006
Award, Best Architects 07, 2007
Nomination, World Architecture Festival, 2008

> Public buildings

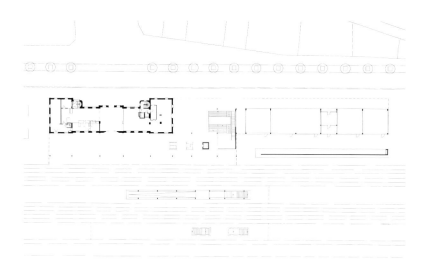

Extension and renovation of the Delémont CFF Train Station, 1999–2004

- 1999 competition, 1st prize

- publications

Le Cahier de la DRA 2006 (August 2006), p. 28.
L'Hebdo, no. 33 (August 17, 2006), p. 52.
Idea, no. 4 (2006), pp. 20–23.
Domobât, no. 1 (March/April 2006), pp. 36–37.
Bâtir, no. 12 (December 2005), pp. 22–23.
AS Architecture Suisse, no. 154 (September 2004).

- Architecture prizes

Prix Wakker CFF 2005
Prix Wakker Delémont 2006
Prix Lignum Jura 2006
Nomination, Distinction Romande d'Architecture 2006

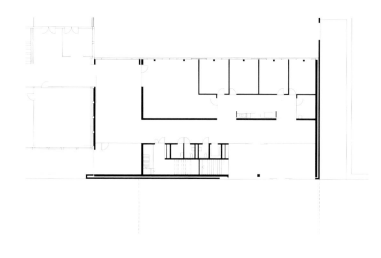

Porrentruy vocational training center extension (Salvi Architecture Sàrl, Kury Stähelin architects), 2001–2004

- 2001 competition, 1st prize

- construction management: Kury Stähelin Architectes SA

- publications:

IIC, Industria italiana del cemento, no. 836 (November 2007), pp. 706–17.
TEC 21, no. 40 (October 2007), p.30.
Architektur neue Schweiz, Veralagshaus Braun, Deutschland, 2007, p. 135.
1000x European Architecture, Veralagshaus Braun, Deutschland, 2006, p. 653.
Domobât, no. 5 (October/November 2006), pp. 10–12.
Bâtir, no. 12 (December 2005), pp. 20–21.
Chantiers & rénovation, no. 10 (2004), pp. 43–46.

Parish renovation in Rebeuvelier, 2001–2005

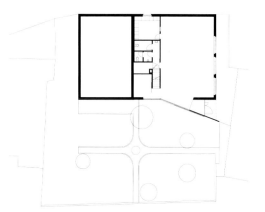

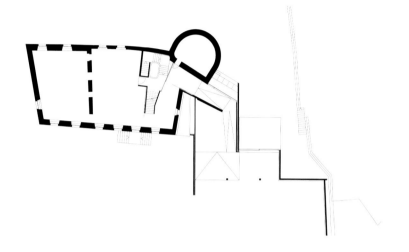

Renovation of a furniture store in Porrentruy, 2006–2009

- publications:
Bâtir, no 12 (December 2009), pp. 9–11.

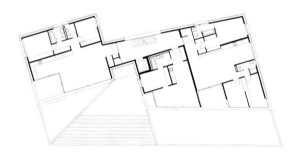

Apartment building in Vaduz (Liechtenstein), 2006–2009

- construction management: P. Konrad, Vaduz

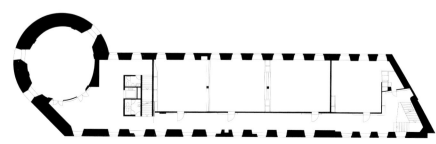

"Le Séminaire" Building rehabilitation, Porrentruy state school extension (Salvi Architecture Sàrl, Romeo Sironi SA), 2004–2010

- 2004 competition, 1st prize
- construction management: R. Sironi SA

> Private villas

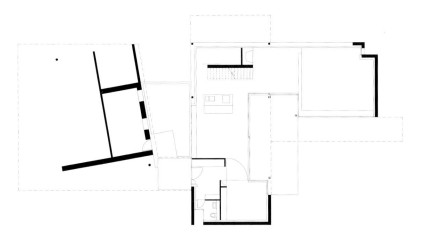

Maître Villa in Develier, 1999–2000

- construction management: R. Voyame.

- publications:

Idea, no. 4 (2004), pp. 14–18.
Maisons et Ambiances, no. 2 (2003), pp. 26–37.
Raum und Wohnen, no. 9 (2002), pp. 34–45.
Bâtir, no. 9 (2001), pp. 22–23.
Hochparterre, no. 11 (2000), p.59.

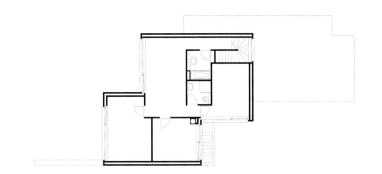

Paumier Villa in Delémont, 2000–2001

- publications:

Maisons et Ambiances, no. 2 (May–September 2005), pp. 24–37.
Raum und Wohnen, no. 1 (2004), pp.40–53.

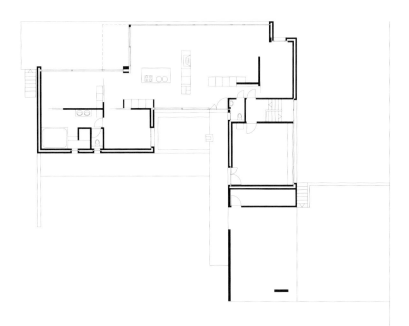

Schaller Villa in Rebeuvelier, 2001–2003

- publications:

Taburet, (May 2006), pp. 152–53.
Idea, no. 2 (2005), pp. 4–8.

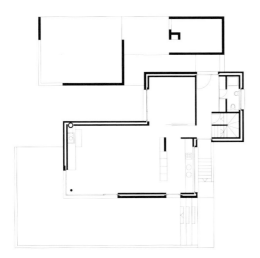

Waldmeyer Villa in Cottens, 2002–2003

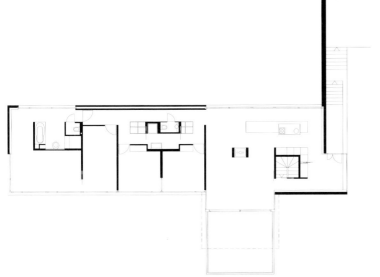

Maitre Villa in Saignelégier, 2002–2004

- publications:

Mercedes Daguerre, ed., *Ville in Svizzera*, Verona: Mondadori Electa, 2010, pp. 142–51.
Maisons et Ambiances, no. 4 (2007), pp. 32–45.
"Ein Haus von ...," lecture at the Institut Architektur, Fachhochschule Nordwestschweiz FHNW, Muttenz, 2006, pp. 40–43.
Raum und Wohnen, no. 12 (December–February 2006), pp. 52–65.
Tendance Déco, no. 2 (May–June 2006), pp. 48–56.
Taburet (May 2006), pp. 154–55.

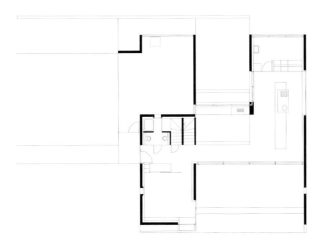

Fleury Villa in Courtedoux, 2003–2005

- publications:

Bâtir, no. 12 (December 2009), pp. 18–19.

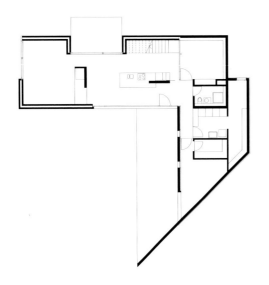

Philippe Villa in Delémont, 2003–2005

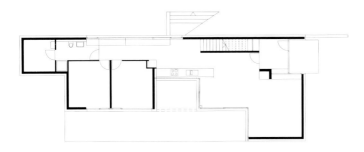

Ruedin Villa in Ayent, 2003–2005

- construction management: d&v Architectes à Sion.

Montavon Villa in Porrentruy, 2003–2005

- publications:

Bâtir, no. 12 (December 2007), pp. 20–21.
GPA, no. 2 (2006), pp. 2, 6–9.

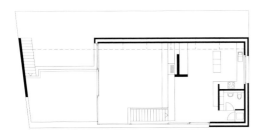

Bastardoz Villa in Cheyres, 2005–2006

- publications :

"Architects Directory 2008," *Wallpaper.com*,
http://www.wallpaper.com/directory/883.
Idea, no. 3 (2008), pp. 42–44.
Dwell 8, no. 10 (October 2008), pp. 80.

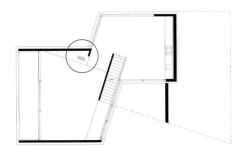

Hillside Villa in Cheyres, 2005–2008

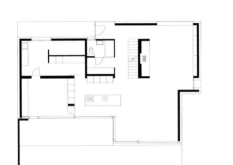

Haefliger Villa in Saxon, 2006–2009

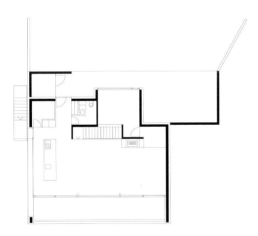

Ehmann Villa in Delémont, 2007–2009

> Renovations

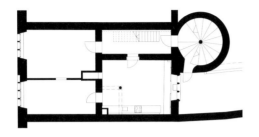

Renovation of a medieval house in Delémont, 2002–2003

- publications:

Le Quotidien Magazine, no. 1 (February 2009, special issue of *Quotidien Jurassien*), pp. 6–7.
Le Temps, supplement, April 23, 2008, pp. 17.
Tendance Déco, no. 5 (November 2006), pp. 64–68.

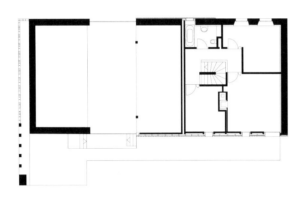

Renovation of an old cottage in Rocourt, 2002–2003

- publications:

Taburet (March 2006), pp. 60–65.
Idea, no. 5 (2005), pp. 26–30.

Private Spa in Mervelier, 2006–2010

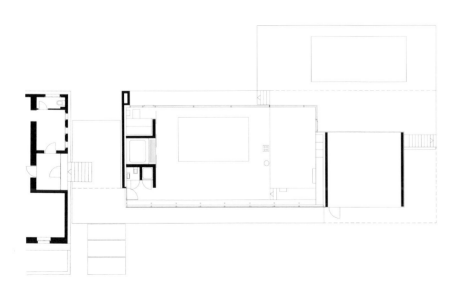

WORKS IN PROGRESS

2005–   Transjurane A16 highway: Civil engineering structures,
         Boncourt-France – Porrentruy West (section 2)
         Transjurane A16 highway: Civil engineering structures,
         Delémont East – Choindez (sections 8)

> Public buildings

2007–   Renovation of the gymnasium in Noirmont
         Invited competition 2007, 1st prize

> Private villas

2009–   Steulet Villa in Rossemaison

2009–   Fleury Villa in Delémont

2010–   Sasso Villa in Delémont

> Renovations

2003–   Series of renovations for a 19th-century building in
         Auvernier (Broillet family, la Roche 17)

2005–   Series of renovations for an individual 1929 house in
         Porrentruy (Sanglard family, Allée des Peupliers 9)

2008–   Renovation of a medieval house in Porrentruy (Lauber
         family, Rue des Baîches 1)

2009–   Renovation of a medieval house in Delémont (Macchi
         family, Rue du 23 Juin 38)

2010–   Conversation of an old cottage in Pleujouse
         (Aeschlimann-Kradolfer family, Clos vers la Croix 8)

2010–   Renovation and extension of a house in Glovelier
         (Mathias-Simon, Rue de la Pran 14)

2010–   Extension to a 19th-century building and outdoor swimming
         area in Delémont (Pose family, Chemin des Places 19)

COMPETITIONS/STUDIES

2010   Léopard City in Carouge
2010   Secondary school in Bassecourt
2009   Train station agglomeration in Delémont
2008   Feasibility study for an apartment complex in Delémont
        (Girard Salvi architectes)
2008   Fire station in Monthey (Girard Salvi architectes)
2007   SafetyCar Jura motorist circuit study in Vendlincourt
        (Salvi Architecture Sàrl, RWB SA)
2007   Institute for disabled persons in Lavigny (Girard
        Salvi architectes)
2006   "Habiter le centre ancien" housing in Porrentruy
2006   Footbridge in Finges (Salvi Architecture Sàrl, Ingénieur
        INGPHI SA)
2006   Jura Hospital extension in Porrentruy (Mangeat Salvi
        Voyame architectes)
2005   Catholic church in Seon
2005   College extension in Delémont
2004   Primary school in Fiez
2004   RER train station in Riehen
2004   CEVA: Bridge over the Arve and planning for the tunnel
        in Val d'Arve (Salvi Architecture Sàrl, GVH Tramelan SA,
        IUB Ingénierie SA Berne, Biol-Conseils SA)

2003   Centre for Industrial Services in Delémont, 3rd prize
2003   Multiple-use building for Raiffeisen bank in Develier, 1st prize
2002   Housing in Basel (Salvi Architecture Sàrl, Kury Stähelin
        architects), 3rd prize
2001   Vocational training center extension in Porrentruy (Salvi
        Architecture Sàrl, Kury Stähelin architects), 1st prize
2000   Elevator access for the Vorbourg chapel
1999   Renovation and extension of the Delémont traing station,
        1st prize

EXHIBITIONS

2010   "Drôles de lieux", Musée jurassien des arts Moutier,
         June 18 to August 29

2008   "carte blanche 5", Forum d'architectures Lausanne,
         April 11 to May 11

2004   "carte blanche", Musée jurassien des arts Moutier,
         January 31 to April 4

COMPLETED PROJECTS AS HEAD OF THE MSBR OFFICE IN DELÉMONT, 1988–1998

1988–1994   Renovations in the old town in Delémont
            - rue du 23 Juin 13
            - rue de l'Hôpital, rue du Nord

1994–1996   Family homes in Delémont
            - Gigon and Guélat Villas at Creux de la Terre 11 a

1995–1998   SUVA Complex / BCJ Bank in Delémont
            - 1995 competition, 1st prize, Quai de la Sorne 22

1998   Renovation of a tower entrance in Delémont
            - rue du Haut-Fourneau 35

1998   Renovation of a medical practice in Courfaivre
            - Héritier medical practice, Rue Saint-Germain 21

STUDIO COLLABORATORS

Primary collaborators:
Architects: Moldovan Cristiana, Lachat Brice

Other collaborators:
Architects: Beuret Alain, Beuret Gaël, Girard Jean-Claude ,
Girardin Sabine, Joliat Vincent, Robert Vincent, Truffaz Vincent
Architectural draftsmen: Letté Dominique, Willemin Sandhya
Interns: Ali Khan Maneeza, Angaramo Florent, Antoine Pierre,
Ashori Alireza, Baroncea Irina, Baumgartner Maryse, Chaignat
Candice, Chételat Lucile, Colomer Bernardo, Comment Benoît,
Comment Jérôme, Dauwalder Aline, De Angeli Isabelle, Doriot-
Burrus Stéphanie, Durieux Guillaume, Ehrbar Julien, Girardin
Frédéric, Glaus Mathias, Horton Marie-Annick, Iovine Aurelio,
Landry Lea, Lemarchand Soazig, Leuba Coralie, Marting Julia,
Morales Mascarell Sergio, Prima Lanig, Prudat Mariève, Queloz
Barbara, Rebetez Isaline, Robin Simon, Strambini Nicolas
Administration: Burri Emma, Degoumois Christine, Lüthi Stéphanie,
Salgat Silvia

Editor: Bruno Marchand

Texts: Bruno Marchand, Martin Steinmann, Jean-Claude Girard

For all the photographs
© Thomas Jantscher
With the exception of
© Yves André, highway pp.16–17, 29, 31, & 38–39, Ruedin Villa at Ayent pp. 53, 112–113, 114–115, & 119,
Medieval house at Delémont pp. 138 & 139
© Filippo Simonetti, Maître Villa at Saignelégier pp. 52, 98–99, 100–101, 104, & 105
© Erick Saillet, Montavon Villa at Porrentruy p.97

Translation from German into English ("The Repetition of Gestures"): Michael Robinson

Translation from French into English ("The Architect's Audacity", "Anchorage", project texts):
Marlyne Sahakian

Copyediting: Irène Coustel, Sophie Mulphin

Proofreading: Jonathan Fox

Layout, cover design, and typography: Rémi Faucheux, Paris

Lithography: Karim Sauterel, Gollion

Printing and binding: Pressor SA, Delémont

We thank the authors of the texts: Bruno Marchand, Martin Steinmann, Jean-Claude Girard

We thank the following companies for their support:
Batipro SA, wood construction, Cornol and Courfaivre
BCS SA, glass and metal façade design and planning, Neuchâtel
Chaignat Denis, CVS - heating and plumbing, Saignelégier
Entreprise du Gaz, heating and plumbing, Porrentruy
Garage de la Gare, J. Montavon SA, Porrentruy
Lachat SA, concrete – cladding – gravel, Asuel
Laurent Intérieurs Sàrl, Delémont
Meubles Ch. Nicol SA, Porrentruy
Parietti & Gindrat SA, construction firm, Porrentruy
Posé François and Antoinette, Delémont
Riat Serge SA, painting-plaster firm, Porrentruy
Tilleul and Val Terbi pharmacies, Delémont and Courroux
Verres Industriels SA, industrial glass, Moutier

As well as a special thanks to the anonymous donor and
Me Degoumois, law firm and notary, Moutier
Denise and Pascal Ruedin, Ayent
Edith and Jean-Michel Maître, Saignelégier

As well as all of our clients and partners.

With the support of:
ÉCOLE POLYTECHNIQUE FÉDÉRALE DE LAUSANNE (EPFL)
School of Architecture, Civil and Environmental Engineering (ENAC)
Theory and History of Architecture Laboratory 2 (LTH2)

A CIP catalogue record for this book is available from the Library of Congress, Washington D.C., USA.

Bibliographic information published by the German National Library
The German National Library lists this publication in the Deutsche Nationalbibliografie; detailed
bibliographic data are available on the Internet at http://dnb.d-nb.de.

© 2011 Birkhäuser GmbH, Basel
P.O. Box, CH-4002 Basel, Switzerland   www.birkhauser.com

This book is also available in the original French language edition by Infolio Publishers, Gollion,
Switzerland (ISBN 978-2-88474-453-9)

Printed on acid-free paper produced from chlorine-free pulp. TCF ∞
Printed in Switzerland, Pressor SA, Delémont

ISBN 978-3-0346-0689-9   9 8 7 6 5 4 3 2 1

BRUNO MARCHAND | ***Der Wagemut des Architekten***
Gespräch mit Renato Salvi

9:18 Uhr, der ICN 617 in Richtung Basel hält in Delémont, der Hauptstadt des Schweizer Juras, nachdem er die eindrücklichen Schluchten bei Moutier passiert hat, an deren steil abfallenden Flanken noch ein paar Nebelschwaden hängen.

Nach einer kurzen Strecke durch eine triste, nichtssagende Ebene gestaltet sich die Ankunft im Bahnhof dafür umso abwechslungsreicher: Der Abgang von den Perrons mündet in einer erstaunlich hellen Unterführung (dank dem raffinierten Verschieben der Passerelle, welche die beiden Perrons verbindet). Die Passage ist seitlich begrenzt durch geneigte, mit Blech verkleidete Seitenwände und oben gefasst von einer Decke, die mit einer minimalen Raumhöhe von knapp zwei Metern extrem tief liegt.

So werden die Schritte des Besuchers von diesem «eingegrabenen», sich längs entwickelnden Raum geleitet, seitlich erhellt von horizontalen Lichtbändern, die sich an Wänden und Decke reflektieren. Beim Hinaufgehen in die Bahnhofshalle bin ich ein kurzen Moment überrascht und beeindruckt von einem hohen Raum unter einem weiten Metalldach, der modelliert wird von luftigen, bequemen Treppenläufen in Richtung Stadt oder Perron 1.

Es ist nicht üblich, dass sich der Bahnhof einer kleinen Stadt eine richtige Architektur-Promenade leistet, ja, eine Promenade, die urban wird und sich unter einem annähernd 80 Meter langen Dach Richtung Parkplätze verlängert. Hier können die Reisenden ihre Einkäufe erledigen oder vor den Schaufenstern flanieren. All diese Räume und Einrichtungen von hoher Qualität wurden vom Architekten Renato Salvi entworfen, der mich in Delémont, wo er sich niedergelassen hat, zu diesem Gespräch empfängt.

Bruno Marchand – *Was hat dich veranlasst, nach Delémont zu ziehen?*

Renato Salvi – Ich bin ein wenig per Zufall in Delémont gelandet, wo ich mich 1988 definitv niedergelassen habe, nachdem ich zusammen mit Flora Ruchat-Roncati den Wettbewerb für die Autobahn Transjurane gewonnen hatte. Allerdings legte nichts in meinem Werdegang einen solchen Schritt nahe. Ich habe italienische Wurzeln und bin in La-Chaux-de-Fonds geboren – einer ziemlich strengen, asketischen, nördlich geprägten Stadt, die mir gut entspricht. Mein Vater ist in den 50er Jahren als Maurer in die Schweiz emigriert, meine Mutter war Uhrenarbeiterin: In diesem familiären Umfeld lernte ich sowohl die harte Realität der Baustellen als auch die Geduld und Genauigkeit verlangende Präzisionsarbeit des Uhrenmachens kennen.

BM – *Kontext und Familie waren gleichermassen prägend ...*

RS – Genau. Man kann amüsante Parallelen feststellen. Der Kontext ist derjenige einer Stadt, deren Kraft von der Repetition kommt: die identischen Fenster, die identischen Treppenhäuser, die identisch ausgestatteten Küchen usw. Andererseits haben wir

die demontierbaren Bauteile der Uhr, die oft ebenfalls identisch und repetitiv sind. Die Wiederholung scheint das Stichwort zu sein: die Uhrwerke sind immer dieselben, basierend auf einer gewissen Anzahl Bauteile. Es sind die Variationen in den Uhrwerken, die bestimmend sind für diesen oder jenen Typ von Uhr.

BM – *Dein Entschluss, in Zürich zu studieren, führt dann aber zu einer Veränderung.*

RS – Mit dem Wegzug an die Eidgenössische Technische Hochschule Zürich (ETH) 1981, um Architektur zu studieren, wurde ich zum ersten Mal mit einem kosmopolitischen Umfeld konfrontiert, und vor allem entdeckte ich dort eine intellektuelle Welt, zu der ich sehr schnell Affinitäten feststellte, obwohl ich dem Einfluss Aldo Rossis, der noch spürbar war, gewissermassen «entkommen» bin. Ich gestehe, dass dieser für mich nicht wirklich fassbar war.

An der ETH fand der Unterricht im ersten Jahr bei Bernhard Hoesli statt. Er hat mit seiner Einführung in die Moderne mehrere Generationen geprägt. Seine Art, diese Themen anzugehen, war mir sehr vertraut. Ein entscheidendes Erlebnis hatte ich aber im dritten Jahr: die Massaufnahmen der Medina von Fez für die UNESCO während fünf Monaten unter der Leitung eines Gastprofessors, Stefano Bianca. Damals habe ich diese unglaublichen marokkanischen Städte entdeckt. Gleichzeitig war es eine Einführung in die vernakuläre Architektur und in eine andere Kultur, die auf anderen Werten basiert.

Schliesslich war aber der Unterricht bei Flora Ruchat sicher ein zentraler Punkt meines Studiums. In ihrer Wahrnehmung der Dinge und der Architektur verbindet sie eine rationale Haltung mit einer humanistischen Denkweise. Ich erinnere mich noch an ihre Beschreibung über das Pflanzen eines Obstgartens in Form eines Fünfecks, damit jeder Baum besonnt ist. Hinter ihren scheinbar harmlosen Äusserungen steckt immer etwas Erfinderisches, und das ist Flora, wie ich sie liebe und immer geschätzt habe. Diese Affinität hat übrigens dazu geführt, dass ich nach dem Diplom während fast vier Jahren in ihrem Büro in Rom gearbeitet habe. Daneben besuchte ich mit viel Ausdauer und Interesse einen Kurs über Restauration, obwohl ich gestehen muss, dass dieser für meine Karriere nicht prägend war.

BM – *Was bedeutete für dich dieser Aufenthalt in Rom?*

RS – Sicher eine Rückkehr zu den Ursprüngen und eine Art, meine Wurzeln wieder zu entdecken, zu meinem eigenen Erstaunen. Ich habe noch lebendige Erinnerungen an die spezielle Stimmung eines in Sonnenlicht getauchten italienischen Platzes, an das Warten auf einen Bus neben einem archäologischen Park oder an das Entdecken von Fresken in einer Kirche. Aber auch an das Gefühl, zum ersten Mal einer undogmatischen Moderne gegenüber zu stehen, die frei ist in der Wahl der Materialien und ihrer Verarbeitung, wie die Architektur von Luigi Moretti. Eine irritierende Persönlichkeit, mit einer gewissen Fähigkeit, in frühere Zeiten zurückzuspringen. Seine Werke aus den 30er Jahren faszinieren mich. Er hat sich aber auch in den 50er Jahren für gewisse Aufgaben unglaubliche Freiheiten genommen, und dies nach einem Gefängnisaufenthalt. Das ist verrückt, seltsam.

BM – *Es war also eine Rückkehr zur traditionellen Architektur, begleitet vom Interesse für moderne italienische Werke, insbesondere für die Komplexität der von Robert Venturi thematisierten Architektur von Luigi Moretti?*

RS – Ja, die sichtlich komplexe Palazzina Il Girasole interessiert mich tatsächlich. Mir gefällt aber vor allem der Gedanke, darin eine Art sinnliche Architektur zu sehen. Eine von Materialien, Texturen und im Licht immer wieder wechselnder Stimmungen geschaffene Sinnlichkeit. Eine Sinnlichkeit, wie man sie spürt beim Berühren einer Betonmauer von Scarpa. Diese Geste löst bei mir immer ein starkes Gefühl aus. In diesem Zusammenhang erinnere ich mich an Bernhard Hoesli, wie er leicht über den rohen Beton von La Tourette streicht und uns ermahnt: «Pläne zeichnen genügt nicht, man muss die Materie berühren!» Scarpa bewegt mich auch durch den Bezug, den er zur Landschaft und zu den natürlichen Elementen herstellt – ich denke da an die Mauer des Friedhofs der Familie Brion in San Vito d'Altivole, die genau so hoch ist wie die Spitzen der Maiskolben im Feld nebenan – oder durch seinen raffinierten Umgang mit Details.

BM – *Gibt es andere Referenzen, von denen du dich inspirieren lässt?*

RS – Einerseits muss ich Alvaro Siza erwähnen, den ich als Student entdeckt habe und der mich schnell fasziniert hat mit seinen Arbeiten, die fast ikonenhaften Vorbildcharakter haben, wie das Schwimmbad von Leça. Auch seine Sozialwohnungen von der Bouça in Porto mit der dichten Aneinanderreihung der Aussentreppen bieten ein noch nie dagewesenes Bild, das etwas unglaublich Lebendiges und Faszinierendes hat, mit all den Leuten, die die Treppen auf und ab gehen. Andererseits ist da auch Alvar Aalto, dessen Werk ich später besucht habe, auf einer Reise mit Jean-Claude Girard, der damals mit mir arbeitete. Ich bin sehr froh, Aalto besichtigt zu haben, als ich schon, in Anführungszeichen gesprochen, reif war. Denn seine Architektur ist nicht leicht fassbar, vor allem wegen der Fülle von Materialien, die er verwendet und auf seine ganz eigene Weise kombiniert, ja «aufeinanderprallen» lässt, in einer Art von Kreativität, die fast ein wenig verwirrend sein könnte, es aber de facto nicht ist.
  Diese beiden Architekten hören natürlich sehr stark auf die Natur und die Landschaft, ein Thema, das mich ganz speziell interessiert und mich nochmals zurückkommen lässt auf meine Wurzeln und auf die italienischen Landschaften: zurückkehren in mein Dorf, die ganze, grosse Poebene durchqueren, am Fuss von Bergamo mit seiner Altstadt ankommen, ins Dorf, in die Hügel hochsteigen, dort eine andere Vegetation vorfinden, das Weiche dieser Landschaft, verglichen mit den Schweizer Wäldern entdecken usw. In dieser Wahrnehmung der Landschaft liegt vielleicht etwas Stimulierendes.

BM – *Kommen wir auf deinen Werdegang zurück. Es scheint mir offensichtlich, dass er, verglichen mit demjenigen der meisten Architekten deiner Generation, untypisch ist, da du praktisch zehn Jahre damit verbracht hast, oder sogar mehr als zehn Jahre, die Transjurane, dieses riesige Infrastrukturprojekt, nach dem Wettbewerbssieg 1988 mit Flora Ruchat zu zeichnen und umzusetzen. Dadurch wurdest du wirklich sehr direkt mit der Landschaft konfrontiert.*

RS – Ja, die Planung und Realisation der Transjurane war tatsächlich während zehn oder etwas mehr Jahren fester Bestandteil meines Alltags, wodurch meine Tätigkeit als Architekt gewissermassen «eingefroren» wurde. Während dieser Zeit hatte ich ganz einfach weder die Zeit noch die Energie, mich anderen Baustellen zu widmen oder mich mit anderen Architekturaufgaben zu befassen. Die Transjurane war aber ein aussergewöhnliches und spezielles Erlebnis, denn es ging nicht unbedingt um eine räumliche Auseinandersetzung, sondern vielmehr um die Kunst, Objekte in der Landschaft zu platzieren, was diesen wiederum eine eindeutig skulpturale Dimension verleiht – eine prägende Erfahrung, die mich nicht loslässt, seit ich mich 1988 selbständig gemacht habe.

BM – *Lass uns über genau diese Frage der Form und ihres Stellenwerts in deinen Projekten sprechen.*

RS – Es gibt einen Satz von Marguerite Yourcenar, den ich sehr gernhabe: «Aber ich, ich bin sehr wohl gezwungen, mich mit der Form zu beschäftigen, sie ist es, die mich von meinem Hund unterscheidet.» Ich gehöre zu einer Generation von Architekten, die es erlebt haben, dass über lange Zeit jegliches Streben nach Form heftig gegeisselt wurde. Ich habe mehrere Jahre gebraucht, um mich von diesem Druck zu befreien, was eigentlich paradox ist, denn für jeden Architekten ist der formale Ansatz primäre Voraussetzung für seine Arbeit, was ihn sicher in die Nähe der Bildhauerei rückt. Für mich war die Arbeit an der Autobahn der Schlüssel dazu, denn da hatte ich Gelegenheit, sehr skulpturale Objekte zu realisieren, die jedoch nicht unbedingt autonom sind, denn ihre Form ist von verschiedenen Parametern bestimmt wie dem Kontext, die Fonktion usw. Aber nicht nur …

BM – *Dieses Thema des formalen Ausdrucks scheint mir in deinem Werk tatsächlich durchgehend präsent und somit auch das Bindeglied zu sein zwischen dessen infrastrukturellen und architektonischen Seiten. Dies vor allem in der Suche nach klaren, einfachen, aber in ihren Aussagen radikalen Formen – ich denke da besonders an die Schule in Porrentruy mit ihren beiden auskragenden Seitenwänden aus Sichtbeton oder auch an die mächtige Auskragung der Terrasse des Einfamilienhauses in Saignelégier.*

RS – Ja, das ist richtig, ich versuche immer die präziseste Form zu finden, vor allem in Bezug auf die Landschaft. So entsteht ein Dialog, manchmal mit erstaunlichen Aspekten: Wenn ich an die Villa Montavon denke, da durchdringt nicht die architektonische Form die Landschaft, sondern vielmehr die Landschaft das Haus. Ich denke auch viel über die Beziehung zur Landschaft nach, wenn es um das Verankern meiner architektonischen Objekte im Gelände geht. So gesehen ist die kleine Mauer des Einfamilienhauses Paumier, die sich auf Bodenhöhe weiterzieht und den Garten einfasst, fundamental.

BM – *Trotz seiner scheinbaren Zerbrechlichkeit verleiht dieses Bauteil dem Haus eine eindeutige Kraft.*

RS – Ich bin froh, dass du den Begriff der Zerbrechlichkeit erwähnst, denn ich glaube, es gibt tatsächlich fragile Aspekte in meiner Architektur, zumindest scheinbar fragile, denn es ist vielleicht genau dieses Paradoxe, das ihr eine gewisse Kraft verleiht. Ja, erstaunlicherweise. Ich denke in diesem Zusammenhang an das Haus Dessaules mit seinen Mauern, die aus dem Boden wachsen, bei Null beginnen, aufsteigen, Haus werden, sich sukzessive zum Vordach wandeln, zur Eindeckung usw. Wenn man diese Mauern vor Ort sieht, wirken sie gleichzeitig fragil und sehr kräftig.
  Aber auch die Autobahn hat eine zerbrechliche und eine kräftige Seite, was mit der Alterung immer besser sichtbar wird. Das Thema des Alterns, auf das ich in Italien gestossen bin, finde ich besonders inspirierend. Ich liebe diese zeitliche Dimension, die dem Offensichtlichen entgegenwirkt: Betrachtet man die Thermen des Caracalla in Rom, spürt man das Gewicht

der Zeit, aber gleichzeitig ist das alles unglaublich zeitgenössisch. Anderseits finde ich die Spuren der Zeit wunderbar, wie auf der Autobahn bei les Gripons, wo Moos wächst und wo wegen der Bäume praktisch alle Mauern rötlich geworden sind, wie eisenhaltiges Gestein.

BM – *Was beschäftigt dich sonst noch im Projektstadium?*

Ich widme mich intensiv dem Zugang zum Gebäude, den ich wie in einer Art Kamerafahrt betrachte, die folgendermassen beschrieben werden kann: Du näherst dich, lässt den Eingang nach und nach auf dich wirken, trittst unter das Dach, entdeckst das Licht … Anderseits, und dies hat wieder mit der Landschaft zu tun, versuche ich beim Setzen des Gebäudes immer, den Boden praktisch nicht zu berühren und es auf den Zentimeter genau zu platzieren.

BM – *Schaut man sich alle Häuser an, die du gebaut hast, stellt man fest, dass es keine wiederkehrende Sprache gibt, obwohl verputzte Mauern und Sichtbeton vorherrschen.*

RS – Für mich ist die Materialwahl nicht vorgegeben und kann je nach Umständen variieren. Nehmen wir den Fall des Einfamilienhauses Paumier. Ich habe es mir lange in Sichtbackstein vorgestellt, vielleicht weil Jean-Claude Girard und ich von einer Reise nach Dänemark zurückkamen, stark beeindruckt von der Architektur Arne Jacobsons. Schliesslich wurde es weiss verputzt, vor allem aus finanziellen Gründen. Sicher, ein Sichtbacksteinhaus wäre in dieser Landschaft fantastisch gewesen. Aber es hätte nicht in den jurassischen Kontext gepasst, wo man traditionsgemäss nicht mit Backstein baut.

Es stimmt, ich versuche in erster Linie ein Gefühl für die Masse und die Schwerkraft zu bekommen. Es ist interessant, denn ich glaube, ich habe nur einmal in meinem Leben eine Stahlbaukonstruktion gezeichnet, als Student. Ich habe eindeutig das Gefühl, diese Technik nicht zu beherrschen, und dass ich sie nur für etwas Vergängliches anwenden könnte … Die Masse, die, einmal mehr, zu meinen Ursprüngen führt, ist für mich notwendig. Einerseits, um diese sinnliche Seite in der Architektur, von der wir vorher sprachen, wiederzufinden – vor allem auch, was die akustische Wahrnehmung betrifft – anderseits, um mit dem Gegensatz der räumlichen Introversion und Extroversion arbeiten zu können, ein Phänomen, das für meine Werke oft typisch ist.

BM – *Was bedeuten dir die andern Bereiche der Kunst, wie die Malerei oder die Bildhauerei?*

RS – Tatsächlich sprechen mich ein Bild oder eine Skulptur oft fast mehr an als Architektur. Im Grunde genommen brauche ich ein künstlerisch-kulturelles Umfeld für meine Inspiration als Architekt. Letzten Sommer war ich in Matera. Da habe ich die höhlenartigen unterirdischen Kirchen entdeckt mit stark byzantinisch beeinflussten Fresken, die mich zutiefst bewegt haben. Diese Bauten stehen da seit Jahrtausenden, und du hast eine Art Christus, der dich immer noch teilnahmsvoll anschaut. Und man weiss immer noch nicht, wer das gemalt hat, wie es dazu gekommen ist, weshalb es geschehen ist, weshalb dort, wie es gemacht wurde. Du stösst dort, in einer Freske auf einem Stück Wand zuhinterst in einer Grotte auf ein tiefes, grundlegendes Bedürfnis, etwas zu zeigen, das weiter reicht als dein Menschsein.

Zoran Music ist ein Maler, den ich sehr schätze. Er hat in Konzentrationslagern gelebt und ist vor ein paar Jahren gestorben. Er zeichnete dort auf kleinen Fetzen Papier haufenweise Körper. Dank einem Bleistiftstummel und einem Stück Papier hat er es geschafft, im schlimmstmöglichen Grauen zu überleben. Andere Maler faszinieren mich nicht nur wegen der

Kraft ihres Strichs, sondern auch wegen der Kraft der Farben. Ich denke vor allem an die sizilianischen Landschaften von Nicolas de Staël, wo er mit nur drei oder vier Farbtönen ergreifende Effekte erzielt. Ich könnte auch Coghuf nennen, einen jurassischen Bildhauer und Maler, den ich ganz speziell schätze. Ich muss gestehen, dass ich zur zeitgenössischen Kunst den Anschluss nicht gefunden habe, sie bewegt mich nicht unbedingt. Ich finde sie jedoch interessant als intellektuelle Vorgehensweise, die mir Horizonte öffnet und mich auf andere Gedanken bringt, ausserhalb der festgetretenen Pfade.

Um auf die Beziehungen zwischen den Kunstdisziplinen zurückzukommen: Die Malerei scheint mir für die Architekten lebenswichtig, denn sie sucht nach dem Ausdruck der Dinge. Mir scheint, dass sich die Architekten über die Zeichnung ausdrücken, und dass du, je besser du zeichnest, desto eher eine gewisse Realität erfassen kannst. So gesehen kann man davon ausgehen, dass der gekonnte Umgang mit Grundriss, Schnitt usw. entscheidend ist für das Schaffen von interessanten Objekten.

BM – *Wenn man von Kunst spricht, könnte man auch von Literatur sprechen.*

RS – Es ist klar, dass die Lektüre auch eine Inspirationsquelle ist, vielleicht, weil sie immer Stimmungen liefert, die man in den Bau einer Mauer oder in den Plan eines neuen Ortes übertragen oder einbringen kann. Marguerite Yourcenar beeindruckt mich, wenn sie von Malerei spricht und diesen Bauern beschreibt, der vor einem Christus von Rembrandt zu beten beginnt. Wenn ich eine Ausstellung konzipieren müsste, sähe ich sicher dieses Bild und diese Beschreibung vor mir, weil dies bei mir all die Fragen des menschlichen Befindens, der menschlichen Existenz aufrührt.

Die Lektüre hilft mir, in mich einzudringen und in meinem Innern vergrabene Dinge zu suchen, von denen ich das Gefühl habe, sie nicht immer fassen zu können. Dies umso mehr, als ich sehr oft nach Fertigstellung eines Objekts den Eindruck habe, nicht ich hätte das realisiert. Ich habe wirklich Mühe mir vorzustellen, dass diese Autobahn ein Werk von mir ist, das ich in so vielen Jahren erschaffen habe, dass dieses Riesending hervorging aus einem Tisch, drei Stühlen und drei in einem kleinen Büro untergebrachten Personen, du siehst … es ist fast ein wenig irreal.

BM – *Beenden wir dieses Gespräch mit einer Aussage des Philosophen José Gil, den du gerne zitierst, sinngemäss: «Das Leben wagen, um singuläre Gedanken zu wagen». Inwiefern kann man bei dir von «wagen» sprechen, vom Wagemut des Architekten?*

RS – Der Wagemut besteht in einer persönlichen Haltung, oft als Reaktion auf die Arbeitsbedingungen. Meine Situation «am Rande» – bezüglich der grossen städtischen Zentren wie Basel, Genf oder Zürich – führt oft zu aller Art von Widerständen, denen der Architekt ausgesetzt ist. Vielfach sind es kulturelle Widerstände, die einem konservativen Milieu entspringen oder einem, das den lokalen Traditionen fundamental verbunden ist.
Wenn ich an die Autobahn denke, besteht das Wagemutige darin, schliesslich der Trägheit der Leute widerstanden zu haben, die sich nicht bewegen oder ganz einfach nichts verändern wollen. Wagemut heisst auch, sich in Frage stellen zu lassen, sich dessen, was man vorschlägt, nicht vollkommen sicher zu sein oder auch an ein langfristiges Projekt zu glauben, wie dies eben bei der Autobahn der Fall ist. Wagemut ist schliesslich auch, nein sagen zu können, nein, ich bin nicht einverstanden mit Ihnen, man muss es anders machen, nicht so. Ich glaube nicht, dass man mutige Architektur machen kann, wenn man im Leben nicht einen gewissen Wagemut an den Tag legt.

MARTIN STEINMANN | *Die Wiederholung von Gesten*
Anmerkungen zur Arbeit von Renato Salvi für die Autobahn durch den Jura

1987 schrieb der Kanton Jura einen Wettbewerb für zwei Portale der geplanten Autobahn, der A 16 aus, welche die verschiedenen Täler des Kantons Jura verbinden wird. Bis zum Bau der Autobahn führten die Strassen über die Höhenzüge, was die Verbindungen und damit die wirtschaftlichen Verhältnisse in den am Rand des Mittellandes gelegenen Tälern erschwerte. Darum würde die neue Autobahn eine Bedeutung haben, die über leichtere, schnellere Verbindungen hinausgeht, sie würde zu einem identitätsstiftenden Werk des Kantons Jura. Als Vorbild gab es den Kanton Tessin: Dort war es gelungen, der Autobahn durch eine einheitliche Gestaltung der Bauten – unter Mitarbeit des Architekten Rino Tami – ein «Gesicht» zu geben. Dort verbindet die Gestaltung die wiederkehrenden Elemente einer Autobahn – die Brücken, die Mauern, die Portale – tatsächlich zu einem viele Kilometer langen Bauwerk.

Eine Autobahn ist aber nicht nur ein grosses Bauwerk, sie ist auch eine grosse «Maschine»; das erkennt man auf den Baustellen, bevor die ganzen Einrichtungen unter Beton oder Erde verschwinden und gerade noch grün markierte Ausgänge etwas von den Stollen und Installationen ahnen lassen, die der Betrieb einer Autobahn erfordert. Es gibt aber auch Massnahmen, die sich unmittelbar auf die Gestaltung der Portale auswirken. Eine von ihnen soll etwa verhindern, dass die Abgase, welche die Autos aus dem einen Tunnel drücken, in den anderen Tunnel zurückgedrückt werden. Diesem Ziel dient die Mauer von einer bestimmten Länge, welche die zwei Seiten der Autobahn noch im Freien trennt und somit Teil des Portals ist. Davon ist noch zu reden. Doch kehren wir zum Wettbewerb zurück.

Renato Salvi, Sohn eines eingewanderten italienischen Maurers, seit wenigen Monaten in Delémont angesiedelt, nachdem er in Rom und später in Zürich für Flora Ruchat gearbeitet hatte – auch an der ETH, als ihr Assistent – wurde für eine Teilnahme selektiert, wie auch Ruchat selbst. Um rechtlichen Problemen aus dem Weg zu gehen – sie war an der ETH noch seine Vorgesetzte – entwickelten sie einen gemeinsamen Entwurf, mit dem sie den Wettbewerb gewannen und in der Folge insgesamt drei verschiedene Portal-Typen bauten. Salvi war damals 32 Jahre alt und arbeitete – neben einer Anstellung – in Delémont für die Autobahn; für die Besprechungen mit Ruchat fuhr er jeweils nach Zürich. Ab 1998 war er allein verantwortlich für diese Arbeit, die aber nicht abgeschlossen ist: Noch fehlen einige Stücke der Autobahn, noch wird an zwei Tunnels gebaut ...

Damit will ich sagen, dass die Autobahn Salvis Leben – nicht nur sein berufliches – während 25 Jahren begleitet hat, wenn das letzte Stück in Betrieb genommen wird. In dieser Zeit haben sich seine Vorstellungen verändert, verändert haben sich aber auch die Bedingungen seiner Arbeit: Bei den beauftragten Firmen haben Ingenieure gewechselt, er musste immer wieder versuchen, seine Ideen zu erklären, ausserdem waren für die einzelnen Baulose der Autobahn verschiedene Firmen beauftragt, deren Ingenieure eigene Vorstellungen beispielsweise über die Gestaltung einer Brücke hatten ... Wenn man Salvi gut zuhört, in einer Wirtschaft irgendwo in der Ajoie, spürt man durch die Erzählungen über seine Arbeit für die Autobahn hindurch eine gewisse Müdigkeit.

Daneben ist die ganzen Jahre seine andere Arbeit gelaufen, für Aufgaben, die der Jura als Gegend einem Architekten bietet: eine Schule, ein Bahnhof, ein Wohn- oder ein Geschäftshaus und immer wieder Villen, die eine ganz andere Detaillierung verlangen als die Bauten der Autobahn, wo alles eingeschränkt

ist auf eine einfache, dem Ingenieurbau entsprechende Gestaltung. Und doch spielt auch dort der Wechsel der Schalungstafeln – beim Wechsel eines Bauloses – eine Rolle. Salvi weist mich auf einer Baustelle darauf hin. Er verletzt die Wirkung der seitlichen Mauern als etwas Ganzes. Sicher, wer mit 100 km/h aus dem Tunnel fährt, sieht die Veränderung wahrscheinlich nicht, aber ich verstehe seine Enttäuschung: Es bedeutet eine Verletzung des Konzepts. Und darum geht es bei seiner Arbeit für die Autobahn in erster Linie: um ein Konzept, das mit wenigen «Wörtern» oder Formen die Bauten als zusammengehörig erkennbar macht.

1988 stiess ich zum Kollektiv, das in Genf die Zeitschrift *FACES* herausgab. Die Zeitschrift wurde damals neu organisiert und das erste Heft – no. 11, 1989 – galt dem Thema «Autoroute», angeregt durch den eben entschiedenen Wettbewerb für vier Portale der in Planung begriffenen Autobahn durch den Jura. In einem kurzen Beitrag habe ich damals versucht, einige Entwürfe unter den Termini «Form» und «Zeichen» zu kategorisieren, wobei die Vorschläge der Arbeitsgruppe Ruchat und Salvi, die den 1. Preis erhielt, in die Kategorie Form – im Sinn von «bonne forme», also Gestalt – fielen. Damit habe ich gemeint, dass diese Portale nicht auf vertraute Bauwerke anspielen, um einen Sinn zu vermitteln, sondern dass sich der Sinn unmittelbar aus der Form ergibt: als ihr Ausdruck.

Davon ist zu sprechen, wenn es um einige Portale der A 16 geht, auf die ich mich in meinem Text beschränken werde, als erstes das Portal mit Ziel, das mit dem Wettbewerb verfolgt wurde. Es wurde, im gleichen Heft, vom Kantonsarchitekten so umschrieben: Auf die Frage, ob es darum gehe, die Bauten im Sinn einer «Familie» zu gestalten, sagte Berry Luscher: «Die Idee einer Verwandtschaft zwischen allen Teilen scheint mir eine starke Idee ...» Das betrifft einerseits die Sicht von aussen, von anderen Strassen aus – «wie im Tessin sieht man von der Kantonsstrasse aus die Bauten von Weitem» –, andererseits die Sicht des Automobilisten, also gewissermassen von innen. «Wir haben eine Art Pascalscher Wette gemacht: Sieht der Automobilist die Autobahn, und wie sieht er sie? Wir haben uns dann gesagt, und darin besteht die Wette, dass die Wiederholung von gleichen Gesten schliesslich bewirken wird, dass er sie sieht.» Die Formen, die man beim Fahren en passant wahrnimmt, würden sich also durch die Wiederholung zu einem Eindruck der Strasse als Ganzes zusammenfügen.

Für den Wettbewerb entwickelten Ruchat und Salvi einen Typ, der in unterschiedlichen Geländen zu verwenden wäre. In den Erläuterungen schrieben sie: «Die Studie versucht ein formales und strukturales Prinzip zu bestimmen [...] für die Gestaltung der betroffenen Orte. Sie löst die Liste der Probleme folglich nicht von Fall zu Fall.» Das Prinzip bestand darin, die Teile – Portal und Zentrale – zusammenzufassen, um damit Wirtschaftlichkeit und Einfachheit zu erreichen und die Zahl der Eingriffe in die Landschaft klein zu halten. Die Grundlage des einheitlichen Portals beschrieben sie so: «Ähnliche technische Bedingungen für alle Zentralen, Lüftung von gleicher Grösse, Lärmschild von gleicher Grösse. Der Typ Terri bildet die Grundlage, nur die Lüftung ist betroffen [Gemeint ist: vom wechselnden Gelände, M.S.]. Kompaktes System der Lüftung, Freiheit in der Neigung des Systems entsprechend dem Gelände.»

Der Wettbewerb galt den Tunnels von Mont Terri und Mont Russelin, deren Portale in Geländen mit sehr unterschiedlichen Eigenschaften liegen: Zum einen im felsigen Hang von

Les Gripons, zum anderen in einem sanften Hang, wie er an der A 16 die Regel ist. Die eingereichten Modelle zeigen die Zu- und Abluftkanäle der Zentrale zu einem flachen Körper verbunden, der sich wie eine Mütze schräg über die zwei Tunnel senkt. Im einen Fall legt sich dieser Körper an den Hang an, im anderen ragt er schräg aus dem flachen Hang heraus, in einem Winkel, der von der Topografie abhängt. Mit diesem «Typ Terri», der entsprechend dem Gelände variiert werden sollte, versuchten die Architekten dem Ereignis des Tunnels eine expressive Form zu geben. Er wurde in der weiteren Arbeit aber aufgegeben, zugunsten eines Typs, bei dem die Teile getrennt sind. Dieser sollte die Grundlage für die weiteren Portale bilden, ausser für den Kessel von Les Gripons, wo die Ein- und Ausfahrten von St-Ursanne eine Art Carrera-Rennbahn im Massstab 1:1 bilden.

In der gebauten Form besteht der «Typ Terri» aus seitlichen Mauern, die mit dem Hang ansteigen bis zur Decke über den zwei Tunnels. Auf diese Mauern ist eine «Rinne» gesetzt, die sich gegen oben verbreitert, dort im rechten Winkel abbiegt und die Stirne dieser Decke bildet. Die Mauer zwischen den Tunnels setzt etwas tiefer an, sodass die «Rinne» sie zusammenfasst. Die Zentrale aber wächst in einiger Entfernung wie eine seltsame Blüte aus der Wiese. Dieser Typ kann verwendet werden, wenn die Tunnels nebeneinander ansetzen. Das ist aber nur an zwei Orten der A 16 der Fall. Sonst sind sie gegeneinander versetzt, weil die Autobahn schräg auf den Hang trifft. Für diese Portale waren andere Lösungen zu finden, wie die weitere Entwicklung von Salvis Arbeit für diese Autobahn zeigt. Sie sind einfacher, was nicht nur topografisch bedingt ist, sondern auch wirtschaftliche Gründe hat. Sie sind aber auch stärker, finde ich.

Wenn man auf den Schweizer Autobahnen fährt, muss man Luscher Recht geben: Sie sind in der Regel erbärmlich, zum einen, weil sie aus zusammenhangslosen Entscheidungen bestehen, weil sie sich also einer Verwandtschaft der Formen verweigern, zum anderen, weil sich die Entscheidungen in der Regel auf das technisch Notwendige beschränken. Es wäre verlockend, an dieser Stelle die Wirkung von Portalen zu vergleichen, von blossen, aus dem Fels gebrochenen Löchern über Röhren aus Stein oder Beton bis zu den Portalen der Autobahn in der Leventina, die alle in steilem, felsigem Gelände liegen, mit vorspringendem Auflager der Fahrbahnen, flachen Decken und seitlichen Mauern, die in ein Gitter aus dreieckigen Formen aufgelöst sind. Ihre Wahrnehmung beruht auf Spannungen, die sich aus solchen Formen ergeben.

Spannungen bestimmen auch die Wahrnehmung der Portale der Autobahn durch den Jura, vor allem der Portale, die Salvi allein entworfen hat. Diese sind auf wenige Elemente beschränkt: Böschungen, Mauern, Decken ... Die Elemente haben wegen ihrer grösseren Einfachheit eine stärkere Wirkung als die älteren. Es ist eine Wirkung, die sich der mehr oder weniger entschiedenen Bewegung ihrer Formen verdankt. Die «Rinnen» des «Typs Terri», die wie Karton wirken, wurden durch – scheinbar – massive Keile ersetzt. So weichen die seitlichen Mauern mit Kraft zurück bis zur Decke, deren Stirne sich in zwei Kanten faltet: eine schmale und eine breite, eine, die gegen oben, und eine, die gegen unten, in den Tunnel, gerichtet ist. Mit diesen zwei gegensätzlichen Kräften weist das Portal eine Form oder Gestalt auf, die das Eindringen in den Hang zum Ausdruck bringt, und zwar unvermittelt, eine Form also, die dem Umstand entspricht, dass sie *en passant* wahrgenommen wird.

Die in den Bauten erkennbaren Regeln bestimmen das Gesicht einer Autobahn. «Die Kunstbauten müssen nicht Kunstwerke sein. Das sind sie im Tessin auch nicht. Die Brücken über die Autobahn sind einfache Balken. Aber die Widerlager sind in einheitlicher Weise gestaltet, von einer bestimmten Idee über das Wesen dieser Brücken. So entsteht der Eindruck, dass diese Autobahn eine Einheit schafft. Es ist dieser Eindruck, der wichtig ist, nicht die einzelnen Kunstbauten,» erklärt der Ingenieur Christian Menn im gleichen Heft von *FACES*. Die für den Bau der Autobahn durch den Jura Verantwortlichen stützen sich auf die Gedanken, die im Tessin entwickelt wurden, habe ich damals geschrieben. In diesem Sinn hat das, was sie anstreben, zweifellos eine politische Seite: die Einheit der Gegenden zu bestätigen, durch welche die Autobahn führt. Und der Wettbewerb für die Portale diente eben diesem Zweck: der Autobahn durch den Jura ein eigenes Gesicht zu geben.

Die Portale der A 16 wecken also eine Empfindung von Bewegung. Sie verdankt sich vor allem den Kanten, die in unterschiedlichem Mass geneigt sind, oder besser, die sich neigen, nach vorne oder nach hinten, und damit Spannungen hervorrufen. Nur, wer sieht bei 80 oder 100 km/h etwa die Falte, welche die Stirne der Decke teilt? Und doch trägt sie zum Ausdruck der Autobahn bei, was auch für andere Dinge gilt, beispielsweise für Mauern und Böschungen, die ebenfalls geneigt sind. Sie bilden durch die Wiederholung ihrer Eigenschaften den *basso continuo* der Erfahrungen, die der Automobilist während seiner Fahrt macht. Dabei beruht ihre Gestaltung auf einfachen Regeln. Ihr Zweck ist es, in den Dingen auch die Landschaft anschaulich zu machen, beispielsweise in den auf- und absteigenden seitlichen Mauern der Portale den Hang, dem sie folgen.

Die Portale wirken als Form, habe ich gesagt, nicht als Zeichen. Aber auch ein Zeichen kann nicht darauf verzichten, Ausdruck zu haben. Der Tunnel auf der Strassentafel hat darin Ausdruck, dass sein Bogen sich gegen etwas stemmt. Alles hat Ausdruck, wie Arnheim schreibt, eine Linie so gut wie der menschliche Körper[1], und Ausdruck erfahren wir als Verhalten. Das heisst, dass wir die Eigenschaften einer Form als Kräfte wahrnehmen; Wahrnehmung, bringt Rudolf Arnheim diese Frage auf den Punkt, ist die Erfahrung anschaulicher Kräfte.[2] Den Bogen eines Tunnels – oder des Zeichens dafür – empfinden wir als stabil, die schräge Kante einer Mauer, von der eben die Rede war, aber als labil. Sie neigt sich nach vorne, sie ist von einer Spannung erfüllt, die wir als Bewegung wahrnehmen. Darum hat es eine besondere Berechtigung, wenn Luscher die Portale *des gestes* nennt.

Ein Bau hat eine spontane Bedeutung, wenn er als Form Eigenschaften vermittelt, die für uns relevant sind.[3] Was wäre dann die Bedeutung der nach vorne geneigten Kante im westlichen Portal des Tunnel du Banné, um ein anschauliches Beispiel zu geben? Diese Kante neigt sich nicht nur stark nach vorne, dem Automobilisten entgegen, sie wird nach oben breiter und schwerer, so dass sie umso mehr als heftige Bewegung wirkt. Auf Grund der starken Spannung, die sie als Form aufweist, macht sie den Druck des Hanges anschaulich: als wenn er die Mauer verformt hätte. Tatsächlich ergibt sich Spannung aus der Verformung der einfachsten Form[4], und das wäre hier eine senkrechte Kante. Diese Verformung erfasst auch die Decke über dem Tunnel. Die seitlichen Mauern aber, die gegen die Tunnel hin ansteigen und dabei breiter – und stärker – werden, wirken dieser Bewegung entgegen, so dass die anschaulichen Kräfte schliesslich in ein Gleichgewicht kommen, ohne sich zu annullieren: Sie bleiben als sich entgegengesetzte Bewegungen wahrnehmbar, wenn wir auf das Portal zufahren.

Es würde zu weit führen, nun alle Portale auf die verschiedenen Muster anschaulicher Kräfte hin zu untersuchen, die sie bilden. Diese wenigen Notizen müssen hier genügen, um das entscheidende Mittel klar zu machen, das Salvi benützt, um die Autobahn als dynamisches Ganzes erfahrbar zu machen. Es ist die Form, die von der Vertikalen abweicht, die sich als Schräge nach vorne oder nach hinten und auch zur Seite neigt, mehr oder weniger steil, mehr oder weniger heftig ... Wie gesagt, nehmen wir alle diese Formen als Verhalten wahr; darum benützen wir Verben, um ihre Eigenschaften zu beschreiben, darum haben sie Ausdruck, darum ist Ausdruck – anders herum gesagt – als Modi des Verhaltens zu bestimmen, die sich in der bewegten Erscheinung der Dinge offenbaren, wie Arnheim schreibt.[5]

Man kann einwenden, dass beispielsweise die gegen den Hang geneigten seitlichen Mauern statisch bedingt seien. Zweifellos, Salvi hat diese und andere technische Bedingungen aber in ein Repertoire von Formen eingebunden, das den Ausdruck der Portale als Ganzes bestimmt. Es sind einfache Formen, wie sie auch dem Strassenbau entsprechen. (Im Vergleich zu den ersten Portalen hat eine Radikalisierung stattgefunden.) Salvi verbindet sie zu Bauten, wo sich jeder Teil auf Grund seiner Eigenschaften in die Dynamik des Ganzen einfügt und diese Dynamik erfasst auch die Landschaft, wie ich gezeigt habe, indem wir sie auf Grund dieser Portale bewusster wahrnehmen. In der steil nach oben weisenden seitlichen Wand des Tunnels der Roche St-Jean empfinden wir die Enge der Klus, in der weit nach vorne weisenden Wand des Tunnel von Neu Bois aber die Weite der Ajoie.

Mit einem an sich einfachen Satz von Regeln ist es Salvi gelungen, die Portale in sehr unterschiedlichen Geländen in einer innerlich verwandten Weise zu gestalten. Eine Liste der «Fälle» – es sind vier oder fünf – kann einerseits die Regeln auf-

zeigen, andererseits ihre von den Verhältnissen eines Ortes bedingte Aktualisierung. Dafür ist hier nicht genug Platz. Ausserdem ist die Arbeit auf verschiedenen Baustellen noch nicht abgeschlossen, wie ich am Anfang gesagt habe; auf einigen Feldern, durch die die Autobahn führen wird, steht noch Mais. Das macht, dass ein Text über die Portale – und über die Autobahn als ganzes – im Grund verfrüht ist. Denn etwas kann er nicht herstellen, nämlich die Beziehung von Autobahn und Landschaft, wenn die Baumaschinen abgezogen sind, wenn die Fahrbahnen in der ganzen Länge der A 16 mit Asphalt bedeckt und die Böschungen mit Gras bewachsen sind … kurz, wenn die Autobahn zu einem Teil der Täler geworden ist, die den Jura bilden.

1. Rudolf Arnheim, *Kunst und Sehen – Eine Psychologie des schöpferischen Auges*, Berlin 1978, S. 455
2. Ibid., S. 414
3. Rudolf Arnheim, *Dynamik der architektonischen Form*, Köln 1980, S. 214
4. Rudolf Arnheim, *Kunst und Sehen*, op. cit., S. 430f
5. Ibid., S. 448

JEAN-CLAUDE GIRARD | *Verankerungen*

2008 hielt Renato Salvi ein Referat über sein architektonisches Schaffen im Architekturforum von Lausanne.[1] Dies war die Gelegenheit, das gebaute Werk eines Büros kennenzulernen, das gerade mal zehn Jahre alt war. Die Zuhörer versprachen sich denn auch eine Gesamtschau von seiner Arbeit. Aber schon der Titel der Veranstaltung «Im Alltag Emotionen sammeln, pflücken und geduldig ernten, auf dem Weg zur eigenen Vorstellungskraft» kündigte etwas Eigenartiges an, und Renato Salvi überraschte das Publikum mit einem Vortrag, den man mit «die Ursprünge» bezeichnen könnte. Das heisst, er sprach über seine Vorgehensweise, seine Referenzen als Architekt, anstatt einfach eine Reihe von Bildern seiner realisierten Projekte zu zeigen.

Wenn ich dieses Referat erwähne, dann deshalb, weil ich der Meinung bin, dass es für das Verständnis von Renato Salvis Werk fundamental ist: Ohne vorgefasste Meinung und mit einer Haltung geprägt von Distanz und Neugierde geht er seine Projekte an, mit imaginären Bildern aus vielfältigen Referenzen. Er zwingt keine einseitige Sichtweise auf, vielmehr schafft er eine Architektur, die in einem konstanten Dialog das Gedächtnis des Ortes, Elemente aus dem Kontext oder Eindrücke von Reisen, auch scheinbar unwichtige Dinge, integriert. Auf dieser vielfältigen Basis realisiert er seine Projekte.

Jenseits der Material- oder Formenwahl bildet meiner Meinung nach dieses Bedürfnis nach einer mehrfachen Verankerung das Fundament des architektonischen Schaffens von Renato Salvi.

Dialog mit dem Kontext

«Ich glaube zutiefst an die Vorstellung, dass das Umstossen dessen, was uns gegeben ist, grössere Auswirkungen hat.» Renato Salvi

Bei der ersten Art von Verankerung geht es um eine kontext- und landschaftsbezogene Haltung, die einige ab 2000 realisierte Einfamilienhäuser besonders gut illustrieren.

Das erste dieser Serie ist das Haus Paumier, das im Jahre 2000 oberhalb von Delémont gebaut wurde. Es ist ein verputzter zweigeschossiger Backsteinbau, teilweise unterkellert, in einem leicht abfallenden Gelände mit einem schönen Blick aufs Tal. Der Gebäudegrundriss besteht aus einer Überschneidung von zwei Rechtecken, sodass in der Diagonalen eine Weitsicht entsteht, die einen grosszügigen Raumeindruck erweckt, trotz relativ bescheidener Abmessungen. Bei diesem Bau wurde der Topografie des Grundstücks sehr grosse Aufmerksamkeit geschenkt, denn das Haus ist so ins Terrain gesetzt, dass jede unnötige Erdbewegung vermieden werden konnte. Dies illustriert eines der Anliegen Renato Salvis, für den die Dinge ihre Daseinsberechtigung haben; wird etwas hinzugefügt, muss es in Verbindung mit dem Bestehenden geschehen. Diese Haltung wird unterstrichen von der kleinen Mauer der Terrasse, welche die Südfassade seitlich verlängert und eine enge Verbindung zum Ort herstellt. Trotz ihrer scheinbaren Zerbrechlichkeit wird sie zu einem fundamental wichtigen Element, dank dem das Haus seine Präsenz auf dem Gelände behaupten kann.

Für das Haus Maître in Saignelégier, 2004 gebaut, bezog sich Renato Salvi beim Setzen des Gebäudes auf das, was man die Mikrogeografie des Ortes nennen könnte. Das Sichtbetonhaus basiert auf einem rechteckigen, eingeschossigen Grundriss (mit Ausnahme einer teilweisen Unterkellerung). Nur die auskragende Terrasse tritt aus dem Volumen heraus. Im Gegensatz zu andern Einfamilienhäusern, und da keine Nachbarbauten vorhanden waren, konnte Renato Salvi die Räume mit einer geschosshohen Fensterfront grosszügig zur nahen Umgebung öffnen. Besondere Aufmerksamkeit galt hier der Beschaffenheit des Terrains, denn auf der einen Seite des Hauses verläuft der Waldrand, auf der anderen breitet sich das grossartige Plateau der Freiberge aus. Der Weg von der Strasse zum Eingang bietet gleichzeitig Anlass, die für die Region charakteristische Geologie und Vegetation kennenzulernen: Diese Thematik findet ihre Fortsetzung im Innern des Hauses mit dem

Felsen, der während der Bauarbeiten zum Vorschein kam und als malerischer Hintergrund für das Esszimmer und das Elternbad belassen wurde.

Von einer ganz anderen Strategie bezüglich der vor Ort angetroffenen Elemente zeugt das Einfamilienhaus Montavon in Porrentruy. Auch sein Grundriss basiert auf einem Rechteck, aber diesmal berührt das Haus den Boden nur teilweise, dank einer Tragstruktur in vorgespanntem Sichtbeton, die beidseits des Hauses eine Auskragung ermöglicht. Die Lage in einem Quartier mit sehr dichter Nachbarschaft liess den Bezug zur unmittelbaren Umgebung nicht zu. Auf diese Tatsache reagierte Renato Salvi, indem er die Landschaft in der Ferne suchte und diese gewissermassen ins Hausinnere holte. Die zweigeschossige Auskragung im Süden öffnet sich ganz auf die entfernte Landschaft. Sie bewirkt eine Loslösung (im wörtlichen wie im übertragenen Sinne) von der unmittelbaren Umgebung und schafft so Privatsphäre. Damit auch das Esszimmer, das sich auf der Strassenseite befindet, von diesem gerahmten Ausblick profitiert, fügt Renato Salvi im oberen Geschoss einen Patio ein in Form eines aus dem Volumen geschnittenen Aussenzimmers, das die Räume auf der ganzen Hauslänge miteinander verbindet. Die Stärke dieses Eingriffs besteht darin, dass mitten im Haus ein Spiel mit komplexen Wahrnehmungen entsteht, hervorgerufen von Reflexionen und Durchblicken zwischen der Architektur und der Landschaft des Tals, die nun mit dem Haus unzertrennbar verbunden ist.

Auch das Einfamilienhaus Ruedin arbeitet mit einem Element der fernen Landschaft, aber diesmal wirkt sich die Natur direkt auf die äussere Form aus, genauer gesagt, auf die Dachneigung. Steht man hinter dem Haus, verläuft das schräge Dach genau parallel zur Bergsilhouette auf der anderen Seite der Rhôneebene und schafft quasi ein visuelles Echo. So verbinden sich die beiden Elemente Architektur und Natur im Massstab des Tals miteinander und sind Teil derselben Landschaft.

Die Reiseeindrücke

«Wenn man reist und in visuellen Dingen Übung hat: in Architektur, Malerei oder Plastik, so schaut man mit seinen Augen und zeichnet, um die gesehenen Dinge ins Innere, in die eigene Geschichte einzufügen.» Le Corbusier[2]

Der Bezug zum Ort wird manchmal bereichert von auf Reisen gesammelten Eindrücken, die das Projekt auf anderen, eher imaginären Ebenen verankern, wie die folgenden vier Beispiele zeigen.

Das erste ist das 2005 in Cheyres errichtete Einfamilienhaus Bastardoz. Die Grundrissform ist hier sehr einfach, sie basiert auf einem Rechteck. Um von der prächtigen Aussicht auf den Lac de Neuchâtel und die Weinberge profitieren zu können, entwickelt sich der Gebäudeschnitt über drei Ebenen, das «Hauptgeschoss» mit Wohnraum, Esszimmer und Terrasse zuoberst. Das Haus funktioniert als Stützmauer und lehnt sich an das stark geneigte Terrain an, während beim Eingang ein dreigeschossiger Aussenraum geschaffen wird, um die drei Ebenen miteinander zu verbinden. Dieser Raum ist eine direkte Anspielung auf ein Haus – quasi eine Ruine – aus den 1930er Jahren, auf das Renato Salvi in der Provinz Bologna gestossen ist und von dem er ein paar Aufnahmen gemacht hat. Fasziniert davon, wie sich die Natur über Öffnungen in den Mauern und im Dach breit macht, übernimmt er dieses Prinzip, um das Haus Bastardoz in die umgebende Vegetation einzubinden. In dem Moment, wo man das Tor durchschreitet, das zum Hautpeingang führt, manifestiert sich der im hinteren Teil der Parzelle gelegene Wald und begleitet einen ins Haus. Auch hier, wie beim Haus Paumier, entsteht der Bezug zum Terrain über einen der Endpunkte des Gebäudes. Diesmal jedoch durch einen Luftraum, denn der Architekt verlängert nicht das Haus, sondern höhlt das Volumen aus und entmaterialisiert buchstäblich die eine Gebäudeseite. Damit sucht er, vielleicht unbewusst, diesen Zustand des Zerfalls, dem er auf dem Lande in Italien begegnet ist.

Das Maison dans le coteau, ebenfalls in Cheyres, gleich unterhalb der Villa Bastardoz, weist durch das in Grundriss und Schnitt versetzte Volumen einen viel organischeren Grundriss auf, was im Innern einen grossen räumlichen Reichtum erzeugt. Man wird dabei an das Organische in gewissen Grundrissen von Alvar Aalto erinnert oder an das komplexe Innere gewisser Bauten Alvaro Sizas, in denen der Raum zum Hauptthema wird. Eine andere, direktere Referenz manifestiert sich jedoch in Form von zwei grossen Mauern, die scheinbar aus dem Boden wachsen. Diesmal handelt es sich um einen ländlichen Bau, den der Architekt 2005 auf einer Reise in Sizilien entdeckt hat und der hier Inspirationsquelle war und ins Projekt einfloss: Eine Umfassungsmauer entlang der Grenze wird immer höher und wandelt sich zur eigentlichen Fassade. In diesem Projekt findet man dieselbe Lust, Elemente zu schaffen, die das Haus deutlich gegen sein Umfeld abgrenzen. Die Verankerung im Gelände geschieht mit zwei mächtigen Mauern, die vom Boden ausgehend in einer leichten Steigung höher werden, bis sie Brüstung sind und schliesslich als Fassadenmauer enden.

Es lohnt sich, auch das Haus Schaller genauer anzuschauen, das 2003 in Rebeuvelier errichtet wurde und am Dorfrand, an der Grenze zur Landwirtschaftszone liegt. Das kultivierte Land reicht bis an die Parzellengrenze, und man sieht, dass Renato Salvi als Höhenreferenz für das Haus die Höhe gewählt hat, die das Korn einmal im Jahr erreicht, bevor es gemäht wird. Dies ist eine Anspielung an ein Projekt des italienischen Architekten Carlo Scarpa, genauer an den Friedhof Brion, wo die Spitzen des Getreidefeldes nebenan die Höhe der Umfassungsmauer bestimmen. Hier wird das Vorbild etwas freier interpretiert als beim Maison dans le coteau, denn Renato Salvi kehrt den Bezug Natur – Architektur um. Das Projekt von Scarpa benutzt das Getreide als Mauerkrone, während das Haus Schaller auf einem Pflanzenteppich zu schweben scheint, was dem Gebäude Fragilität und Leichtigkeit verleiht.

Mit dem Projekt für die Erweiterung der Berufsschule in Porrentruy muss Renato Salvi in einen Kontext von Bauten aus verschiedenen Epochen eingreifen. Die ersten entstanden in den 1980er Jahren, eine Hierarchie ist nicht zu erkennen. Er entschliesst sich, die Erweiterung in der Fortsetzung des Hauptgebäudes zu platzieren, und gibt so dem Komplex wieder einen Kopf, mit einem Gebäude, das zur Hälfte aus einer Auskragung für den gedeckten Pausenplatz besteht. Mit der Kraft der seitlichen Mauern hätte das Ganze gewissermassen als vom Vorhandenen komplett losgelöste Hinzufügung verstanden werden können, vor allem aufgrund der Materialisierung und der Positionierung senkrecht zum Bestehenden. Um dies zu verhindern, hat Renato Salvi ein künstliches Bindeglied entworfen, ein Element, das aussieht, als wäre es vorher gebaut worden, und das ihm als Anknüpfungspunkt dient. Dieses Vorgehen ist vermutlich von einem anderen römischen Vorbild inspiriert, von Il Girasole des Architekten Luigi Moretti. Dieser, enttäuscht, dass auf dem Grundstück seines Gebäudes keine Ruinen gefunden wurden (was in Rom fast immer der Fall war), beschloss, falsche zu zeichnen, als Fundament für sein Projekt. So hat er sich die Freiheit genommen, sich die Bedingungen, die er brauchte, selbst zu schaffen. Renato Salvi macht dasselbe, indem er mitten vor der Fassade des bestehenden Gebäudes ein Betonvolumen platziert (den Nebeneingang), das sich in Form einer langen Sitzbank, ebenfalls in Beton, bis zur neuen Erweiterung zieht. So werden die zusammengewürfelten Bauten auf dem Gelände miteinander verbunden, mit einem Eingriff, der nicht auf dem Bestand beruhte.

Das Gedächtnis des Ortes

«Die Geschichte als Erhellung.» Renato Salvi

Schliesslich sprechen wir noch von einer anderen Form der Verankerung: das Gedächtnis des Ortes aufspüren, ein Vorgehen, das vielen Projekten, vom öffentlichen Gebäude bis zum Umbau, inhärent ist.

Der SBB-Bahnhof in Delémont ist die erste grosse städtische Intervention des Büros, entstanden aufgrund eines im Jahre 2000 gewonnenen Wettbewerbs. Dieses Projekt bot die Gelegenheit zur Auseinandersetzung mit einer so wichtigen Schnittstelle wie einem Bahnhof, dem eigentlichen Eingangstor zur Stadt. Die erste Massnahme bestand im Wegräumen aller im Laufe der Zeit sukzessive zugefügten Elemente, um so dem Hauptgebäude seine ursprüngliche Silhouette wieder zu geben. Nur die Eingänge wurden in einer zeitgenössischen Sprache neu gestaltet. Der Abbruch des ehemaligen Garderobentrakts ermöglichte den Bau eines langen Gebäudes mit Läden, das über ein Vordach mit dem Altbau verbunden ist. Die Situierung des Neubaus im Grundriss ist insofern sehr präzise, als die Breite des abgebrochenen Gebäudes übernommen wurde. Zwischen diese beiden Eingriffe legte der Architekt den Zugang zur Unterführung, die zum Herzstück des Ganzen wurde, denn dort treffen Alt und Neu auf eindrücklichste Weise zusammen. Führte vorher eine bescheidene Treppe auf die Perrons, so findet man dort heute einen zweigeschossigen Raum vor, von dem aus Treppen zu den verschiedenen Bereichen des Bahnhofs führen. Dieser Raum in Sichtbeton schiebt sich unter die typisch schweizerische Bahnhofsbedachung aus getöntem Holz und gestrichenem Metall, als wollte er das Dach nicht berühren, sondern es vielmehr durch den Kontrast der Materialien hervorheben. Der Eingriff ist bewusst einfach gehalten, ohne übermässige finanzielle Mittel realisiert und bewirkt durch die Kombination der vorhandenen Elemente, alter und neuer, eine Vereinheitlichung aller Interventionen.

Bei der Renovation des kantonalen Gymnasiums von Porrentruy zeigt sich der Wunsch, «die Geschichte als Erhellung» als Stimulans für die Vorstellungskraft zu benutzen und daraus eine Interventionsstrategie zu machen. Hier wird der ehemalige Betrieb eines Seminars in Erinnerung gerufen, vor allem in den Korridoren, entlang derer die neuen Klassenzimmer aufgereiht sind. Die in den tiefen Mauern versenkten Fenster schaffen Nischen, in denen sich die Schüler hinsetzen und lernen können. Sie sind nur neu in Stand gesetzt und liegen gegenüber einer Serie von Holzpaneelen, in die nicht nur die Korridorbeleuchtung, sondern auch die Türen der Klassenzimmer integriert wurden. Die Lern- und Studieratmosphäre wird durch Elemente geschaffen, die beim Besucher den Eindruck erwecken, in ein fast klösterliches Universum einzutreten, und die Erinnerungen an Türen von Mönchszellen in gewissen Klöstern wach werden zu lassen. Um diese Atmosphäre noch zu verstärken, wurde die alte Kapelle am anderen Ende des Gebäudes nur einfach renoviert. Zwischen den beiden Endpunkten hat der Architekt die Elemente der vertikalen Erschliessung platziert, in einer durchwegs zeitgemässen Sprache, die mit den alten Materialien verschmilzt.

Bei einem Umbau, den er für sich selbst vornahm, in einem Gebäude des 16. Jahrhunderts in der Altstadt von Delémont, arbeitete Renato Salvi mit punktuellen Interventionen im Raum und verzichtete auf einen kompletten Umbau, aus «Respekt vor den Vorfahren». Er nahm sich gewissermassen zurück und setzte aus dieser Haltung drei Elemente, ohne jedoch die Spuren der Vergangenheit und die von den vorherigen Bewohnern hinterlassenen Geschichten anzurühren. Eine Treppe, eine Küche und ein Durchgang zur aussen gelegenen Galerie sind die einzigen Eingriffe, mit ihnen konnten die aktuellen Bedürfnisse der neuen Eigentümer abgedeckt werden. Alle übrigen Elemente wurden nur restauriert.

Eine andere Haltung zeichnet den Umbau des Bauernhauses mit angebauter Scheune, das Haus Kaufmann, in Rocourt aus. Das Innere war schon zahlreichen Umbauten unterzogen worden und befand sich in sehr schlechtem Zustand, es gab tatsächlich kein einziges Element, das erhaltenswürdig gewesen wäre. Um mit dem neuen Eingriff trotzdem an den alten Ort zu erinnern, wurde das Innere vollständig ausgeräumt und neu ausgebaut, aber mit einem Masssystem, das die Proportionen der früheren Räume übernimmt. So konnten mit dieser Typologie die Bedürfnisse der Bauherrschaft berücksichtigt werden, vor allem mit dem Einbau einer offenen Küche und den ineinanderfliessenden Räumen im Erdgeschoss, während die vom Massstab der Räume generierte Atmosphäre, vor allem die lichte Raumhöhe, die Bewohner daran erinnert, dass sie in einem alten Bauernhaus wohnen, trotz zeitgenössischer Materialien und Raumeinteilung.

Ein Umbau aus jüngster Zeit, den das Büro realisiert hat, befindet sich ebenfalls in Porrentruy. Es ging darum, den Möbelladen Nicol in der Altstadt zu renovieren, der in den 80er Jahren komplett neu wiederaufgebaut worden war. Der damalige Architekt hatte sich für eine Architektur «im alten Stil» entschieden, das heisst, für versetzte Volumen mit unterschiedlich geneigten Dächern. Weil er jegliche Illusion vermeiden wollte, hat Renato Salvi das repräsentativste Element, die Volumetrie, erhalten, um dann radikal einzugreifen, indem er den ganzen Gebäudekomplex mit einer vertikalen, unterbrochenen Holzlattung verkleidete. Die äussere Form wird damit zum vorherrschenden Element, das sich mit den Nachbarbauten verbindet und seine Zugehörigkeit zum Ensemble ausdrückt, ohne jedoch die Andersartigkeit zu verleugnen. So entsteht ein Spiel mit der Wahrnehmung, indem die «falschen alten» Elemente eine Nebenrolle spielen und je nach Position des Besuchers unterschiedlich in Erscheinung treten. Im Innern wurden ein paar punktuelle Eingriffe vorgenommen, um wieder an gewisse vorhandene Elemente anzuknüpfen, vor allem an den rückseitigen Garten, der beim Wiederaufbau vollkommen vernachlässigt worden war. Eine Fassade wurde herausgeschnitten und einfach auf den Boden gekippt, sodass daraus eine Terrasse entstand, die sich zum dahinter gelegenen Schloss öffnet. So ist die Verbindung wieder hergestellt, mit einer gewissen historischen Ehrlichkeit.

Mit diesem Gang durch einige Bauten von Renato Salvi habe ich versucht, einen Schlüssel für deren Lektüre zu finden und das Thema der Verankerung zu erläutern, das mir für das Entziffern seines Werks wichtig scheint. Es wurde gezeigt, dass dieses Thema in Variationen vorkommt, sei es im Zusammenhang mit Elementen des Kontexts, mit Reiseeindrücken oder dem Gedächtnis des Ortes.

Die auf einer Reise, beim Lesen oder in einer Landschaft gesammelten Impressionen und Bilder stimulieren eine Einbildungskraft, die ihren Ausdruck in seinen Realisationen auf unterschiedliche Weise findet. Dabei ist speziell interessant, dass Renato Salvi mit diesem Vorgehen Quellen vermischt, Kontext, verschiedene Epochen, die a priori nichts miteinander zu tun haben. Indem er es fertig bringt, diese zusammenzuführen, schaltet er gewissermassen die geografischen, kulturellen und historischen Grenzen aus und schafft neue Bezüge. Wir haben einen fundamental dem Kulturellen verpflichteten Architekten vor uns, stellt er doch mit seiner Entwurfsarbeit Verbindungen jenseits aller Grenzen her, seien sie physischer oder psychologischer Natur.

Es ist in diesem Sinne, dass Renato Salvis Arbeit zu uns spricht, durch seine Fähigkeit, Quellen zu vermischen, um seine Projekte besser zu verankern und sie so zu einem Teil eines grösseren Ganzen werden zu lassen.

1. *Forum d'architecture*, Carte blanche 5, 10. April 2008
2. Le Corbusier, *Mein Werk*, aus d. Frz. v. Lilly v. Sauter, Niggli, Teufen 1960 (Hatje Cantz, Ostfildern 2001), S. 37 (frz. original: *L'Atelier de la Recherche patiente*, Vincent & Fréal, Paris 1960)

Übersetzung aus dem Französischen («Der Wagemut des Architekten», «Verankerungen»): Virginia Rabitsch